Bronx Banter

LASTING YANKEE STADIUM MEMORIES

Unforgettable Tales from the House That Ruth Built

EDITED BY

Alex Belth

FOREWORD BY YOGI BERRA

SPORTS
PUBLISHING

For Todd Drew

Sports Publishing books may be purchased in bulk at special discounts for sales promotion, corporate gifts, fund-raising, or educational purposes. Special editions can also be created to specifications. For details, contact the Special Sales Department, Sports Publishing, 307 West 36th Street, 11th Floor, New York, NY 10018 or sportspubbooks@skyhorsepublishing.com.

Sports Publishing® is a registered trademark of Skyhorse Publishing, Inc.®, a Delaware corporation.

Visit our website at www.sportspubbooks.com.

10 9 8 7 6 5 4 3 2 1

Library of Congress Cataloging-in-Publication Data is available on file.

ISBN: 978-1-61321-237-0

Printed in the United States of America

CONTENTS

Foreword ix

Introduction xi

TODD DREW 1

RICHARD BEN CRAMER 5

JANE LEAVY 7

PAT JORDAN 14

PETER RICHMOND 18

JOHN SCHULIAN 20

BILL NACK 24

PETE HAMILL 30

RAY ROBINSON 34

BOB COSTAS 38

ALLEN BARRA 42

DAVID ISRAEL 45

VIC ZIEGEL 50

MAURY ALLEN 51

GEORGE KIMBALL 53

LEIGH MONTVILLE 62

TOM BOSWELL 65

ED RANDALL 71

WILL WEISS 75

ED ALSTROM 78

DAVE KAPLAN 82

ALAN SCHWARZ 85

KEN ROSENTHAL 88

JOHNETTE HOWARD 89

BOB KLAPISCH 92

ANTHONY McCARRON 96

DAVE KINDRED 98

MIKE VACCARO 101

PETE CALDERA 104

JOE POSNANSKI 106

STEVE RUSHIN 109

JEFF PEARLMAN 111

DAVE ZIRIN 113

MAGGIE BARRA 115

MARTY APPEL 118

BRUCE MARKUSEN 120

DIANE FIRSTMAN 122

HANK WADDLES 125

JAY JAFFE 129

STEVEN GOLDMAN 133

JON DeROSA 138

JONAH KERI 142

ROB NEYER 145

NATHAN WARD 150

DAYN PERRY 153

SCOTT RAAB 155

JOHN C. McGINLEY 157

LUIS GUZMAN 159

CONTENTS

CLIFF CORCORAN 162
JOSH WILKER 166
CHARLES PIERCE 172
KEVIN BAKER 176
MARK LAMSTER 180
GLENN STOUT 184
EMMA SPAN 187
TONY KORNHEISER 191

THE NEW STADIUM: FIRST IMPRESSIONS

ALEX BELTH 197
NEIL DEMAUSE 204
TYLER KEPNER 208
MARILYN JOHNSON 210
TED BERG 212
MARSHA DREW 215

Afterword: Additional Memory 219
Contributors 223
Acknowledgments 237
About the Editor 239

As someone who grew up in Baltimore, asking for fond memories of Yankee Stadium is like asking Saint Peter to wax sweetly on Hell. The only good thing that ever happened at Yankee Stadium was when the Colts beat the Giants in the overtime game, but, alas, I wasn't there.

— **Frank Deford**

FOREWORD

Everybody's got a memory of Yankee Stadium; how can you not? I've got so many that I've forgotten some. When people ask if I miss the place, it's tough to say. To me, it wasn't quite the same after they remodeled it in the 1970s. All the changes made it a little different than the place we played in.

I guess Yankee Stadium will always be in my heart. I'm sorry to see it over, because it was a big part of our lives. For me it was special and still is. That first time I walked into the park it was breathtaking. The war was over and I was still in the Navy. The place was so vast, like a Grand Canyon for baseball. It was 461 feet to dead center, Death Valley. Capacity was around 65,000. For doubleheaders, we drew even more than that. The only ballpark I'd known was Sportsman's Park in St. Louis, where we went as kids. It was maybe half the size. Yankee Stadium was really different.

When I first visited, I told the clubhouse guys I was going to play here one day. The next year—1946—I got called up from the minors for the last two weeks of the season. That was the first season they played night games at the Stadium. But mostly our games were played during the day. And almost every Sunday, a doubleheader.

Sure I was fortunate. It was my luck that I got to play with some great players, including (Joe) DiMaggio for five seasons. We had pre-war guys like (Charlie) Keller, (Tommy) Henrich, and Phil (Rizzuto). Later it was Whitey (Ford), Mickey (Mantle), Moose (Skowron), and Hank (Bauer).

The Stadium was our home. Our teams were like family and it's where we practically lived. The clubhouse was no plush health club like you have today. We had a locker stall and stool. But it's where we spent so much of our time, playing cards, talking baseball, horsing around.

What do I remember most? Our teams and winning a lot. We had fun and always got along really great. I guess one of my biggest memories is Don Larsen's perfect game. It had never happened before in the World Series, and it hasn't happened since. And it happened against the Brooklyn Dodgers, who had that great lineup. There was a real pressure atmosphere, especially late in the game. You almost felt the crowd's nervousness. Sure it was exhilarating when it was over. That's why I jumped in Larsen's arms. Some people ran on the field, but it was no mob scene. Things were different then. The fans used to leave the Stadium by walking on the field, through the outfield gate.

All in all it was an exciting time playing baseball, especially in New York. Especially in Yankee Stadium. All that history and tradition, where Ruth and Gehrig and others played. Unless you were there, it's hard to explain. The bigness of Yankee Stadium, the memories, the thrills, it was something else. It was a dream.

— **Yogi Berra**
May 2010

INTRODUCTION

Live in New York long enough and you become nostalgic by default. Walking down the city's streets can send me into a daydream in a heartbeat. I'll look up at a storefront and remember seeing the midnight show of *The Rocky Horror Picture Show* at the old New Yorker theater on the Upper West Side; or enjoying a late-night stop to browse for books at Shakespeare and Company (now a drugstore), even if the clerks were pompous and rude. I've never gotten used to the drop in my stomach when I look up to find that yet another familiar sight has been replaced. You know you can't fight the relentless change in the city and that sometimes the new is actually an improvement over the old, but still, part of me always feels sad.

We knew that losing Yankee Stadium, originally opened in 1923 and greatly remodeled in the mid-seventies, was going to be tough. Maybe not as devastating as what happened to the old Penn Station, but significant just the same, especially for generations of Yankee fans. In the communal spirit of my blog, Bronx Banter, I thought it would be fun to run a series celebrating peoples' memories of the place. So in the spring of 2008, I started asking around—bloggers, newspaper beat writers and columnists, novelists and actors—and by October, we had sixty-two pieces.

One of the essays, Todd Drew's "The Memories Will Not Stop," was selected for *The Best American Sports Writing 2009*. It was only the third time in the annual anthology's twenty-year history that a blog entry had been so honored. But there is even more to this story.

Todd popped up on my radar as a commenter on the Banter. Then we started trading e-mails. And then we were friends. He worked for the ACLU, loved the Yankees and sportswriting, and started his own blog, Yankees for Justice. His posts were slices of life, New York scenes that had more in common with Jimmy Breslin and W. C. Heinz than Bill James and Baseball Prospectus. I thought they were terrific and felt that Todd shared my fascination with character and detail and, most importantly, with storytelling. When I moved Bronx Banter from Baseball Toaster to SNY.tv in the fall of 2008, I asked Todd to join us, and after careful consideration, he did.

He wrote a column called Shadow Ball five times a week, short sketches each drawn with an artist's zeal for perfection. He gave them to Michael Allen, his close friend and colleague, for feedback. And then he asked me to read them. Todd did anything he could to make his work better, sharper, truer to his heart.

The first time I read his lasting Yankee Stadium memory essay, I thought, "Ah-ha, this is what this series is all about." The only problem was, Todd wrote his piece in the second person and I'm not wild about the second person. I asked him to try the first person, but when he did I knew instantly that he had it right the first time.

So we ran his original and it made *BASW*, and joy would have graced Bronx Banter if it were not for one thing: Todd didn't live long enough to see his sweet and powerful essay memorialized. In late November, he told me he needed minor surgery, but he didn't anticipate being laid up for long. My gut told me it was more serious than that, but I figured Todd for the kind of guy who wouldn't let on even if that were the case, so I didn't press the issue. On December 22, 2008, Todd wrote what would be his last piece for publication, an essay about how baseball provided him with an escape from tough times. It had helped keep him sane when his father died, and now it was doing the same as he prepared for his own surgery the following day. The essay was, as John Schulian later put it, what Hemingway meant when he wrote about "grace under pressure."

After ten hours of surgery to remove cancerous tumors from his abdomen, a blood clot reached one of Todd's lungs. He was sedated and kept on a respirator in the hopes that he would recover. He was alive for almost another month, his loving wife Marsha at his side as he lay in bed unconscious but for a few precious moments. On the afternoon of January 14, Marsha realized that Todd was not going to make it. Just after midnight, minutes before the end, she took out her iPod, put one earpiece in Todd's left ear, the other in hers, and played jazz violinist Regina Carter's record, "Paganini: After a Dream." Almost as soon as she hit play, Todd opened his bottle-green eyes wide for a few moments and then he was gone. Michael Allen was holding Todd's right hand, Marsha was on the other side of the bed holding his left. Todd died at 12:42 AM on January 15, 2009. He was forty-one.

Gone was a neighbor, a friend, and a brother, a real mensch. I tried to imagine something we could do in Todd's honor. The rest of the Banter writers and I talked about it and Diane Firstman suggested that we compile the Stadium Memories series into a book. When Skyhorse approached us about doing just that, we knew we had the perfect farewell to Todd.

Todd once sent me an e-mail listing some of his favorite journalists. I reached out to those writers, told them about Todd, and asked if they'd be willing to contribute an essay. I heard back from many of them. Some, like John Ed Bradley and Gary Smith, responded immediately, expressing their sympathies, but simply didn't have a memory of Yankee Stadium worth writing about. Others like Dave Kindred, Peter Richmond, Charles Pierce, Steve Rushin, Dave Zirin, and Leigh Montville, came through beautifully—with the generous help of John Schulian, a veteran of both the sportswriting and Hollywood script writing worlds. Through John, we also got terrific original contributions from Tom Boswell, David Israel, George Kimball, and Tony Kornheiser. Richard Ben Cramer delivered one of the best pieces in the series—the only one that was strictly about the New York Football Giants.

What you hold in your hands now is a collection of memories of Yankee Stadium devoted to our man, Todd Drew. It features a full range of experiences about one of Todd's—and our—favorite places. Even though the old Stadium is now gone, it will always remain a part of our memories. The same goes for Todd, whom we love and will remember for the rest of our days.

— **Alex Belth**
April 2010

LASTING
YANKEE STADIUM
MEMORIES

TODD DREW

The memories will not stop. Sometimes they come in the middle of the night and you have to walk. So you head down five flights to Walton Avenue. You pass the spot on East 157th Street where a batboy once found Satchel Paige asleep in his car after driving all night from Pittsburgh.

Memories say it was fifteen minutes before the first pitch when the boy shook him awake. They also say that Satchel asked for five more minutes and then threw a two-hit shutout.

Memories say things like that.

You cut over to Gerard Avenue where a Mickey Mantle home run would have landed if the Stadium's roof hadn't gotten in the way. That's how the memories tell it anyway.

You walk up River Avenue behind the bleachers of the old Yankee Stadium. There will be no more games here, but you keep coming back because this is where your memories are.

You move past the millions that have huddled in the cold and the heat and the rain and sometimes the snow for tickets. The line wraps around the block and down East 161st Street near where a Josh Gibson home run once landed.

Your friend Earl from Harlem carries his father's memory and says that blast may have hit the new Yankee Stadium if it had been across the street back then. Earl says that the new Stadium couldn't have held Gibson any better than the old Stadium. That memory always brings a smile.

You wander down Ruppert Place and away from the new Stadium because it doesn't hold your memories yet.

The players' gate draws you this way. Everyone has walked in and out of those doors, and your friend Henry has seen them all. He is at the Stadium every day just like a lot of other people from the neighborhood.

There was a rainy afternoon last year when everyone else left, and the cops even took down the barriers, but Henry wouldn't leave because Hideki Matsui was still inside. You both got wet and shook Matsui's hand.

You remember standing there all night when the Yankees won the pennant in 2003, and David Wells came out with a bottle of champagne. He offered up drinks, and everyone cupped their hands. The sticky-sweet smell of victory still clings to the scorecard back in your apartment.

You look over at Gate 4A and remember how long this place has been your home. You think about all the wins and the losses, too. Every day at the ballpark is a good one, but the pennants and the World Series titles make them even better.

You dig around your memory and try to find the best. There are lots to choose from, but you settle on one from a few years ago.

A boy and his grandfather were waiting in line at Yankee Stadium. The boy was eighteen and unable to buy beer, so the grandfather had picked up three bottles at a bodega and slipped them under his coat.

"They won't frisk an old man," he said.

The boy rolled his eyes, but the grandfather got through with the beer.

"Two bottles for me and one for the boy," the grandfather said. "He is young and shouldn't drink too much."

"What are we gonna eat?" the boy asked.

The grandfather pulled a big bag of peanuts from his pocket.

"An old man can get away with anything," the grandfather said.

They found their seats and cheered for all the Yankees but saved their loudest for Jorge Posada and Bernie Williams.

"We are all from the same island," the grandfather explained. "The Puerto Ricans will always get my best."

Posada and Williams both hit home runs in the game, and the grandfather was feeling good.

He started eyeing a lady in low-cut jeans and a skimpy top who was sitting in front of him, and when the Yankees stretched their lead in the eighth inning, the grandfather blurted out, "Nice tattoo."

The lady's boyfriend wheeled around and took a swing at the boy. There was a scuffle, and the boy defended himself well. The boyfriend and lady were so offended that they left.

"An old man can get away with anything," the grandfather said again.

"Yeah," the boy said.

"It was a good fight," the grandfather said. "And it's been a damn good game."

The boy stared straight ahead but managed a smile.

The grandfather put an arm around him.

"You're a good boy," he said. "But you gotta protect against the right hook."

They both laughed.

You still see the boy around. He's a man now and can buy beer on his own. His grandfather is gone, but that memory will walk through this neighborhood forever.

RICHARD BEN CRAMER

M y grandfather took me to my first game at the Stadium. Not baseball: the Cleveland Browns against the New York Football Giants. I lived in Rochester and, as a consequence, I was a Browns fan. As to whether this was right and proper, I thought not at all. I knew nothing about sports marketing and could not have cared less if small-market Rochester had been gerrymandered into the Browns' TV-turf as a sop to get the Modells' vote for the television package. I was fourteen, and I loved Jim Brown.

By modern standards, I was still a casual fan. Football was more fun to play than to watch, and I lived in a neighborhood with wall-to-wall kids. There was a backyard game every Sunday, so I probably missed more Browns' games than I saw. But even I knew that this would be a big game: December football; the Browns had to win it to get to the championship. It was also a revenge game: the Giants had beaten the Browns two straight (the final game of the season and a special playoff) to get to the '58 championship, said to be the greatest ever played. I knew the Browns would have beaten the Colts, and, dutifully, I reviled the Giants.

I was stunned by the ballpark. My notion of a stadium was Red Wing Stadium, where the Rochester Triple-A ball team played. But this was something else—vast and powerful, filled with 60,000 thousand fans, and the tangy scent of smoke mixed with alcohol (which I wouldn't smell again until I could go into bars), and noise like I'd never heard in my life. I couldn't even describe the noise—a wailing screech?—ebbing and then rising as loud as a jet plane. I fell silent. I felt tiny.

But the Browns gave me courage. As I remember, the game was tight, with the Browns clinging to a nervous lead by the half—at which point some kind of miracle transpired. Suddenly, the Browns could do no wrong, and for the Giants, nothing went right. Tittle was intercepted for a score. Jim Brown caught a pass and waltzed into the end zone. The Giants fumbled, the Browns scored . . . and again . . . and again . . . and I was whooping and cutting up just as loud as I could, just like the (suddenly silent) New York fans . . . or so I imagined—it only showed how little I understood.

When the Browns' backups scored again, and their score climbed to more than fifty points, I asked my grandfather (rather too loudly) if that big Longines scoreboard could show three digits for the visiting team. A couple of New York fans turned around and gave me the look that was my real introduction to Yankee Stadium. I had known for about the last quarter that they probably wanted me to shut up. But their look now didn't say, "Shut up." What it said was they wanted to kill me. What it said was this was the worst moment of their lives and if I didn't shut up they might forget how unutterably sad they were, and have another drink, and kill me for sure.

I shut up. I feared them. But I also respected them. No one I knew felt that way about their team. And they taught me something important, which was the dire seriousness of New York sports—which is what the old Stadium was about.

JANE LEAVY

May 18, 1962, was a raw spring night in the Bronx. A mean chill filled Yankee Stadium, suppressing attendance at the Friday night game between the Yanks and the Minnesota Twins. A forgotten subterranean tributary of the Harlem River, on whose banks the Stadium was built, runs on a diagonal from left field toward the hole between third and short like a cut off throw. The ancient waterway, Cromwell's Creek, buried deep beneath the sedimentary rock of urbanization, asserted itself in the dew and chill. Mist enveloped the scalloped copper frieze that ringed the upper deck of the Stadium. I remember thinking: If Mick hits one out tonight nobody will ever see it again.

That was the thing about Mantle: you never knew what might happen when he stepped to the plate or what might happen to him.

My father, who grew up on the other side of the Harlem River rooting for the Giants from a rocky perch on Coogan's Bluff, had gotten box seats behind the dugout along the third-base line. It was the best seat I ever had until I gained admission to the press box fifteen years later.

I was ten years old that sweet, overcast evening. For me, it was the ultimate doubleheader—a visit to The Mick and a sleepover at my grandmother's. Her apartment was just up the street in a building called the Yankee Arms, a long, loud foul ball from home plate.

Mickey was my guy but I was grandma's girl, her favorite, I thought, as did each of her seven grandchildren. I knew I was most favored, though because although she preferred rose sachet to pine tar and canasta to baseball, although she was never tempted to cross the Stadium's threshold in the twenty years she lived in its shadow, she nonetheless put on her mink stole and open-toed shoes and took me to Saks Fifth Avenue to buy me my first baseball glove. It was an odd place to go in search of a mitt, but she wanted the best for me.

In my worldview, Celia Zelda Fellenbaum and Mickey Charles Mantle were linked by something far more precious than proximity: They were stoic in the face of pain and selfless in the pursuit of pleasing others. Like The Mick, she played hurt. She had consigned herself to a lifetime of self-administered insulin shots after one too many peach sundaes at the ice cream parlor on 161st Street where Joe D. could be found between ends of a doubleheader. Her illness did not deter her from filling her refrigerator with six packs of Pepsi and baking the seven-layer chocolate cakes and rugelach her diabetes precluded her from eating.

Providence intervened on my behalf at Saks Fifth Avenue. A mannequin in the store window had a Sammy Esposito glove on her hand. "We'll have that one," my grandmother informed the flummoxed salesman, who pointed out it was not for sale. But he was no match for a Jewish grandmother, mine anyway. I took Sammy home; I took Sammy everywhere. I took him to high holiday services at the Concourse Plaza Hotel and to the Stadium on the evening of May 18, 1962, in hopes I might get lucky again.

My grandfather, a manic-depressive immigrant tailor, had made me two identical, wool, plaid skirts, one in tones of beige, brown, and gold; the other in red and green, Christmas-tree green, perfect for Hanukah. They were reversible and indestructible. A whole wardrobe, these skirts. They went with everything and nothing. He was in a manic phase when he sewed them; their oscillating hems reflected his ups and downs.

My mother made wearing one of these atrocities a condition of attending the game. I chose the more muted tones and an overly generous straw-colored Irish cable-knit sweater over a white turtleneck. I looked like a pre-pubescent haystack.

In an act of solidarity for which I remain grateful seven years after his death, my father headed for the nearest concession stand and bought me an adult-size Yankee cap, large enough to hide most of my embarrassment.

I knew it was going to be Mick's year. God owed him, didn't He? After allowing Roger Maris to claim the Bambino's title as home run king in 1961? But playing second fiddle had its advantages and made Mickey more lovable to the fickle masses. I couldn't love him any more than I did already.

"In 1961 I became an American hero because he beat me," he would tell me decades later. "He was an ass and I was a nice guy. He beat Babe Ruth and he beat me so they hated him. Everywhere we'd go I got a standing ovation. All I had to do was walk out of the dugout."

Such was the case when he emerged from the dugout in the bottom of the ninth inning with the Yankees trailing the Twins by a run. With Maris out of the lineup, Mickey was the Yankee offense. In his first three at-bats he had walked twice and scored both times. But in the top of the seventh, when Whitey Ford gave up a two-run home run to Harmon Killebrew to allow the

Twins to regain the lead, my mother announced she had seen enough. I ignored her.

An inning later with the Yankees still trailing 4–3, she gathered her belongings. I pulled my cap lower on my brow, refusing to make eye contact. In the top of the ninth, she stood up—not to cheer but to go.

With the Yanks down by a run and Mickey due up fourth?

She pursed her lips and sat down. The murmuring began when Yogi Berra pinch-hit leading off in the bottom of the ninth—Mickey was at the bat rack. Berra popped out to short. But then Tommy Tresh singled, a measly infield hit to be sure, but enough to get Mick into the on-deck circle. The murmur turned into a thrum. There he was right before my eyes swinging a bat with that graceful torque of possibility. The big blue seven was jumping off his back. No doubt the roar that greeted him could be heard up the street in my grandmother's parlor where she always feared the reconstructed leg of the grand piano would succumb to partisan vibrations.

Joe Pepitone stepped to the plate. He was my mother's favorite, though only because she liked the feel of his name on her tongue—"Pepe! Pepe!" A deep fly ball to center, still Death Valley then, moved Tresh into scoring position and brought Mantle to the plate.

I told you.

Minnesota manager Sam Mele summoned lefty Dick Stigman from the bullpen and ordered him to throw only low curve balls. But the first of them hung perilously high. Mantle mauled it, hitting a vicious grounder to shortstop. Out of the corner of his eye, he saw Zoilo Versalles fumble the ball and reached for a burst of remembered speed.

Mantle collapsed five steps from the bag, having torn the adductor muscle from the bone. He looked like a dancer in mid-leap, his legs extended beyond reach or reason. He hung there for an instant, or so it seemed, before the force of gravity sucked him to the ground, splayed in the base path. "It was like a deer getting shot at mid-stride," the *New York Post* reported the next morning.

He was roadkill.

The time on the big Longines clock in right-center field said 10:23 PM. Everyone in the ballpark stood, all 20,112 of us, including my mother, the one thing he couldn't do. Mantle later told me he never heard a big place get so quiet so fast.

He refused the stretcher proffered by the loyal trainer and was carried from the field on his teammates' shoulders. That fateful early season bouncer to short was emblematic of Mantle—going all out all the time, whether swinging for the fences or hustling down the line. He played so hard he tore himself apart.

Mantle showered on crutches. I limped to my grandmother's apartment in reflexive solidarity. As always, the injury was worse than originally feared. Mantle had injured his left knee, the good one, when he fell. He would never be the same. And the Yankees weren't the same without him.

They lost fourteen of the twenty-eight games he missed. After they beat Willie Mays and the San Francisco Giants in the World Series that fall, Mantle was named the year's Most Valuable Player, the third and last time he won the award. He said Bobby Richardson deserved it more.

My father took me back to the Stadium six years later to say good-bye to The Mick. It was 1968. God was dead; Bobby Kennedy and Martin Luther King had been murdered; my grandmother was buried in a family plot in Queens, hard by the Long Island Expressway. Mickey was on his last legs, getting ready to retire.

I don't remember the date, the opponent, the score. The Senators, perhaps? A Sunday doubleheader? I remember that my father drove me past my grandmother's front window at the Yankee Arms, that he purchased the best seats available, which weren't very good. We sat behind a pillar just to the left of home plate, a field-level box tucked way back in the shadows of the first deck where pigeons made their presence known.

I remember the bolts in the steel girder obstructing my view and a sickly hue of over-painted green. I remember that my feet stuck to concrete suffused with decades of soda pop and cotton candy. I remember the chill of the shadows and how the temperature rose—seemed like 20 degrees—when I stepped into the sun.

I don't remember anything that Mickey did or might not have done. A methodical search of newspaper clipping files and Retrosheet's database has yielded no clues. Memory refuses to give up its secrets.

On Thursday night, September 18, 2008, four days before the last game at the Stadium, I took the D train uptown to say good-bye. I walked up 161st Street past the drugstore where my grandmother got her insulin prescriptions filled, past the former home of the G & R Bakery where a replica Torah once resided behind a glass window above cooling racks of black-and-white cookies. I crossed the Grand Concourse to the Concourse Plaza Hotel where Mickey and Merlyn lived as newlyweds, now a city-run home for senior citizens. I took the elevator to the ballroom level where I attended Rosh Hashanah services with my grandmother and Sammy Esposito. The ballroom was gone. The shofar doesn't sound there any more.

I stood beneath her window at 751 Walton Avenue and decided not to knock on the door of her old apartment and headed for the ballpark. From the upper deck landing by the escalator, I could still see the Yankee Arms.

I expected to be overwhelmed. Or sad. Or something. I felt only hungry—the concession stands were sold out of everything by the seventh inning—and oddly disconnected from the infrastructure of my childhood. Maybe it's because this reconfigured iteration of Yankee Stadium wasn't where Mickey played. It's not where he fell in the outfield in the fall of 1951 and in the base path in the spring of 1962. It's not where I made up my mind that I would go ahead and eat the seven-layer chocolate cake waiting in my grandmother's kitchen despite Mickey's pain. It would have been rude to refuse. Just because he played hurt, why should I suffer?

PAT JORDAN

I was twelve the first time I visited Yankee Stadium in 1953. I had been invited to appear on Mel Allen's pre-game TV show because, as a Little League pitcher in Connecticut, I had pitched four consecutive no-hitters and struck out every batter I faced except two. I arrived in a tan suit and a tie, with my glove in a paper bag. I expected the Yankees to ask me to throw a few, and then sign me to a contract. But they didn't. Mel Allen just talked to my parents, then asked me a question. I mumbled an answer and sulked.

The next time I went to the Stadium was in 1959, when I was seventeen, a star pitching prospect, trying to get the Yankees to give me a bonus. That trip, I remember clearly. The Yankee PR person ushered me and my older brother down to the team's pressroom, which, I was amazed to discover, had wood paneling painted white with blue pinstripes.

Mel Allen was there, again, at a table. He mistook me for Rocky Colavito, the Cleveland Indians slugging outfielder. Why not? We were both Italian. But he didn't remember me from six years before. Then I was led to the Yankees' clubhouse, where all my heroes were in various states of dress. I gawked at my idol, Whitey Ford, with his freckled red skin and blue eyes, smoking a cigarette, reading the *Wall Street Journal*, and

Yogi Berra, squat and homely. Mickey Mantle was straddling the aluminum whirlpool machine. He was amazingly short, I noticed, and tightly muscled. His shoulders and chest, and the thigh and calf of his left leg were wrapped in bandages. He was grinning as I passed. It was a wide, blank grin that lent his puffy face an air of boyish dissipation.

I changed into a Yankee uniform, then left the dressing room and began walking through the darkened runway that led underneath the concrete stands. Above me, I heard a faint rumbling. The runway became darker and darker as the stands above me graded lower and lower, and then suddenly I stepped through a doorway into the Yankee dugout and was momentarily blinded by the flash of sunlight and cloudless sky and immense expanse of field spread out before me. It took me a minute to catch my breath and for my eyes to adjust to the sudden brightness. Then, I traced the towering, triple-decked stands that surround the playing surface everywhere except in center field. As the stands rose they curved away from, then out over, the field, casting a huge shadow, like the wings of a prehistoric bird, across the dark grass. The center-field stands were open to the sun and seemed miles away. Behind them on an elevated track a train passed slowly. Only much later would I notice that the paint on those towering stands was faded and peeling, and that the grass which had looked so green was actually yellowish and did not cleanly outline the base paths as it should have. Yankee Stadium, as I remember it from that day, was not the most beautiful stadium I would visit. But it was the most majestic and the memory of that day still chills me.

As I threw, the Yankee and Kansas City players began to emerge from their dugouts like stragglers from a routed army. They started leisurely games of catch and pepper along the first-base and third-base lines. They joked back and forth across home plate while I threw, unnoticed, between them. I was too scared to look either left or right, so I just continued to throw harder and harder until finally I cut loose with my first full-speed fastball. Johnny Blanchard was catching me. The sound of the ball hitting Blanchard's glove echoed around the stadium. The moment the ball left my hand I knew it was traveling faster than any ball I had ever thrown. I threw another fastball, and another, and another, each one a small explosion of its own. Those tiny explosions so exhilarated me that I failed to notice the Yankee and Kansas City players had also stopped their banter. Nor did I notice when they also stopped their games of catch and pepper to just stand quietly and watch me throw. I was not aware of anything really, except that the ball in my hand was as weightless as Styrofoam and my motion had slipped into a groove so natural and smooth, and mechanically perfect that it required no effort.

The scouts sat behind the home-plate screen while I warmed up on a mound behind home plate. Blanchard turned toward the scouts, said something, and tried to slip a sponge into his mitt without me noticing it. But I did.

After I finished throwing, I showered and dressed and went into the general manager's office where the farm director Johnny Johnston and my brother bargained over my bonus. The guy who had scouted me for the Yankees, Ray Garland, was there too. I sat there silent at a big conference table. The Braves had offered me $50,000, but I desperately wanted to pitch for the Yankees. They offered me $36,000.

"The kid won't sign for a penny less than forty," my brother said. "We know we can get that from any club."

"Maybe," said Johnston. "But the Yankees are not 'any club.'"

Ray Garland stood up. "He's right, ya know. Jesus Christ, this is the Yankees! Most kids would sign with us for nuthin,' much less thirty grand." Johnson nodded and motioned for Ray to sit down.

"It's got to be at least forty," said my brother. "And at that we're willing to take less than we could get from other clubs."

Johnston was silent for a moment and then said, "Three twelves. Thirty-six thousand dollars, and that's our final offer. If you leave here without signing, it's going down to thirty."

I didn't sign and never played in Yankee Stadium, which I had come to see as my rightful baseball home, again.

Years later when I would remind my brother about that day in Johnston's office, he'd say to me, "You know, I really wanted to take their final offer. But I knew it wasn't what you wanted." I said, "But it was! It was what I wanted!" My brother shook his head. "No, it wasn't," he said. "It would have hurt your pride to take less than we planned on."

PETER RICHMOND

Four decades later, memory images shift. The players' faces and names start to blur, rosters blend and mingle; the spasmodic fits of the owner made every new season an unpredictable shifting of the sands. Even the Stadium itself changed shape during Lindsay's renovation. But one thing endures in memory, and always will: the colors.

Not the blue of the pinstripes, or the soft brown of the pitcher's mound dirt, or the emerald of the outfield grass. No: the colors of the DiNoto's Bread sign, painted in the late-fifties onto the side of a brick apartment building beyond right-center field: BUY DINOTO'S BREAD, it read, in yellow letters, atop a field of red, green, and white stripes: the Italian flag. That folksy, personal plea, uttered by a local family business, made my stadium, my refuge, into my home.

It was the mid-sixties when the DiNoto's sign became my own personal emblem, a beacon of greeting that signified the compact between a kid not yet in his teens, but newly old enough to ride the 5 train uptown by himself. I'd been raised in boarding schools. Vacations were spent in one Upper East Side apartment, then another, then another, as my parents marched upward to the most rarefied of neighborhoods. None of them— the schools, the apartments—felt like places I belonged.

But I was at home in the upper deck, with its panoramic view of old buildings that suggested true neighborhoods where people did belong, had roots, had their local team. And every time I went to a game, the DiNotos welcomed me home.

I'd sit in the upper deck, surrounded by a few scattered thousands of diehards like me, seeking their own refuge, I suppose. The team was worse than terrible, but I didn't care. Horace Clarke, Jerry Kenney, and Mike Kekich might have been baseball mediocrities to the experts, but to me, they were heroes. They were my family, playing baseball in my house. And no matter what was happening down on the field (a typical weekend series, faulty memory tells me, would entail my team dropping three of four to the Indians, with Pepitone salvaging the final game with some mighty blast into the black seats), no matter how often the roster shifted, no matter how many games they lost, the DiNoto's sign was there, exactly the same. I could almost smell the bread baking. Someday, surely, the DiNotos, whoever they were, would invite me for Sunday dinner.

When did it disappear? I can't say for sure. All I know is that at some point in the nineties, I went to a game, and the DiNoto's sign had been painted over in white, readying for a new advertisement. I have no idea what the new advertisement might have been selling in those final years. I do know that when the red, white, and green flag disappeared—when the relationship between me and some faceless but surely smiling family of bakers was severed—so were my ties to the team.

Now I have my own home, and my own family. Perhaps some day, in some other dimension, in some other timeless time, I will be breaking DiNoto's bread at their table. For now, though, the sign still glows brightly, welcoming me home.

JOHN SCHULIAN

It's an existential question, I suppose: Do you have to be in Yankee Stadium for the creation of your favorite Yankee Stadium memory? I ask because the memory of the old joint that I cherish most was conjured up in Salt Lake City, which is a long way from the Bronx geographically and even farther in karmic miles.

There I was, thirteen years old and freshly transplanted in Utah's capital from Los Angeles, working off a severe case of culture shock by playing pepper with my new friend Kenny Caputo and his father. I called him Mr. Caputo, but the grown-ups who stopped by his house addressed him as the Sheik, and soon enough I did too. Kenny and I would toss him the ball and he'd rap sharp little grounders back at us with a well-used wooden bat, laughing and shouting that we deserved a chew of tobacco every time one of us snagged a tough one. It was fall and the 1958 World Series was going on, the Yankees in a rematch with the Milwaukee Braves, their conquerors the year before. I may have wondered who would win this time, but the Sheik certainly didn't.

"Them Yanks," he said. "God, they're tough. That Berra, that Mantle—you oughta see 'em."

"Have you?" I asked.

"Hell yeah," the Sheik said. "Me and Kenny both."

Kenny confirmed his dad's claim with a nod.

"The '56 Series," the Sheik said.

He didn't have to tell me what happened in that one. I knew all about Don Larsen's perfect game.

"We seen it," the Sheik said. "We was there for every game."

The Sheik had been an interesting character before this revelation, a bootlegger's son and a semipro first baseman, but now he took on an aura that glowed brighter with every detail of his great adventure. He had never been farther east than Chicago when he and Kenny set out for New York by train, traveling on free passes the Sheik had earned working as a machinist on Union Pacific's steam engines. The fact that he and Kenny didn't have tickets for any games bothered him not a whit. It was the fleabag Times Square hotel where they stayed that tied his stomach in knots. "God, I was so scared, I slept with my pants on," he said. "Anybody broke in, they'd have to cut 'em off me to get my wallet."

The Sheik's pants and wallet survived intact. After that, everything was easy. He and Kenny would buy standing-room tickets from scalpers, and once they were in the ballpark—it didn't matter whether it was the Stadium or Ebbets Field—the Sheik would go to work on the ushers. "They thought I was in the Mafia," he said. Then again, they might have been swayed by the ten-spot the Sheik duked them in exchange for prime real estate. Whatever the explanation, he and Kenny were standing behind the home-plate box seats when Larsen did the impossible and Berra leaped into his arms and the Stadium became, for that one brief instant, the center of the universe.

I've carried the story of how Kenny and the Sheik bore witness to baseball history all these years, as both a source of delight and something against which to measure my own special moments in the Stadium. I made my first visit in 1970 when the Yankees were dreadful and I didn't care because I just wanted to be in the same ballpark as Ted Williams. I'd never seen him play in person, and I'd barely seen him on TV, but by God, I saw him that night when he was managing the Washington Senators and he walked out to home plate with his lineup card.

Came 1977 and I was back in the Stadium, this time as a sports columnist covering the World Series for the *Chicago Daily News*. I got a couple of memories out of that one: Reggie Jackson's three homers in Game 6 being the obvious; lunch with Red Smith, the press box nonpareil, being the sublime. "Oh no," he said when I reached for my wallet. "This is my town."

Subsequent years produced more Stadium memories, but I was never sure which one I cherished most until this past New Year's Day. USC was belaboring Ohio State in the Rose Bowl so I went channel surfing and found the MLB Network making its debut by showing Larsen's perfect game as it was broadcast in '56. Though Larsen and Berra were on hand to answer Bob Costas's questions, I confess that I was more interested in the shots of a crowd dominated by cigar smokers wearing topcoats and fedoras. Kenny and the Sheik were there somewhere—I knew they were—but I never could spot them.

Just the same, I called the Sheik to tell him what I'd seen. "You're kiddin' me," he said. He is ninety-three years old now and still ready to shovel snow at home in Salt Lake or fly to California to visit his daughter. He'll still tell you, too, about the biggest trip of his life, the one that took him all the way to Yankee Stadium. That was what he did this time, though I'd already heard the story a dozen times, maybe more. The Sheik told it just the way he had when I was a kid, never missing a beat, and somewhere between the dumpy hotel room and Larsen's masterpiece, I found myself wishing for the impossible. I wished the Sheik's story would never end.

BILL NACK

On a balmy afternoon in February 1999, as old Yankee Stadium was getting her face lifted and nails polished for the spring opener, I visited the grand old yard to peer into the nooks and corners of her incomparable history and at once found myself standing on the pitcher's mound, turning slowly on the rubber to behold the scene.

Over the years, I had seen and covered many games in this fabled yard, but not until I stood on that elevated mound of dirt—alone on that field, in silence, with only a few pigeons for company—did I fully understand Babe Ruth's two-word exclamation when he first stepped from the dugout at Yankee Stadium and looked up at her distant walls, her tiered seats, her vastness. It was April 18, 1923, the day of the grand opening of the 70,000-seat stadium, and here the Babe declared for the ages: "Some ballyard!"

Writers would soon be elbowing each other aside to find words bold and colorful enough to describe the place and the things that happened within it.

F. C. Lane, in one article, wrote, "From the plain of the Harlem River it looms up like the great Pyramid of Cheops from the sands of Egypt."

It was only 281 feet down the line in left, but from there the wall flared suddenly outward until it rose 490 feet away, in dead center field. Wrote one pop-eyed scribbler for the *New York Sun*: "The flag pole seems almost beyond the range of a siege gun as it rears its height in distant center field."

What a day it must have been in this old house! More than 70,000 people crowded cheek-to-jowl in the stadium on that opening day, and cordons of police ringed the dirt roads around it, at one point forming a phalanx to protect the flinty-jawed new baseball commissioner, Kenesaw Mountain Landis, as he broke through the flivver dust and pushed his way through the gates. On the field, John Philip Sousa led the Seventh Regiment Band in "The Star-Spangled Banner" as the two rival managers—New York's Miller Huggins and Boston's Frank Chance—hauled in the rope that lifted the flag above the center-field fence.

Of course, the Babe had the final word that first day, homering to lead the Yankees to a 4–1 victory over the Red Sox. Not to be outdone, and in the spirit of the day and the occasion, sports-writing immortal Grantland Rice rolled up his sleeves, spit on his hands, and came up with a kind of pear-shaped lead that was nearly as colorful as Ruth himself:

> A white streak left Babe Ruth's 52-ounce bludgeon in the third inning of yesterday's opening game at the Yankee Stadium. On a low line it sailed, like a silver flame, through the gray, bleak April shadows, and into the right field bleachers. And as the crash sounded, and the white flash followed, fans arose en masse . . . in the greatest vocal cataclysm baseball has ever known.

From that mound some seventy-six years later, you could almost see Ruth's silver flame as it streaked out of the infield and toward the seats, until, at last, it gradually resolved itself into a fat, gray pigeon winging down and across the field from the upper deck. Over those seven-and-a-half decades, Yankee Stadium became the richest repository of memories in American sports. This was where heavyweight champion Joe Louis fought eleven times, and it is where, in 1938, in the most politically electrified prize fight in history, the Brown Bomber knocked out Hitler's paragon of Aryan supremacy, Max Schmeling, at 2:04 of the first round.

This was the field where Rocky Marciano, his nose butter-flied like a Benihana shrimp and bleeding profusely, came back in a final, ferocious assault to punch out Ezzard Charles and retain his title. This was the house where Johnny Unitas, on December 28, 1958, in what came to be known as the Greatest Game Ever Played, started on his own 14-yard line and drove the Baltimore Colts down field in the final two minutes of regulation play—throwing one unerring pass after another to flanker Raymond Berry—to set up a field goal that tied the game, 17–17. The Colts then won it in overtime, 23–17.

In the end, though, this was always the House That Ruth Built. Here the Bambino turned the home run into the engine that drove baseball out of the shadows of the Black Sox scandal and into a run of decades in which it grew into the national pastime. Stand on that mound and close your eyes, and you can see them all on a February afternoon.

There is Ruth mincing around the bases on his way to hitting sixty home runs in 1927, and there he is slipping out a door in the right-field fence, between innings, to have a hot dog or three surrounded by fans. There is Lou Gehrig, ailing and tired, listening to the echoes of his own farewell speech in 1939. And there is little Al Gionfriddo, the Dodger left fielder, looking over his shoulder as he miraculously runs down Joe DiMaggio's 415-foot drive in the '47 Series, with Red Barber famously yelling into his radio microphone, "Gionfriddo's going backbackbackback!" As Al reaches and catches it, Barber cries out, "Oh, doctor!"

Of all the baseball played in Yankee Stadium in eighty-five years, nothing matched what happened there on the most memorable night of all, October 18, 1977, when the Yankees, leading the Dodgers three games to two in the World Series, were home to face Los Angeles in the sixth game. Reggie Jackson had been perceived as the villain ever since he showed up at spring training and declared that he, not team leader Thurman Munson, was the man to lead them to their first World Series victory since 1962. "I'm the straw that stirs the drink," Reggie said. "Thurman thinks he can stir it, but he can only stir it bad." That judgment was probably true, but his utterance of it left him ostracized and alone in the Yankee clubhouse, and he spent a good part of the year dodging slings and arrows in the press and fighting with manager Billy Martin. So, Jackson came to the sixth game of the '77 Series still suffering through what had surely been his longest season. Of course, as things turned out, October was his glass, the World Series was his drink, and no one in the annals of baseball ever stirred it better.

Stand on that mound, and you can replay it swing by swing.

In the fourth inning, with the Yanks losing 3–2 and with Munson on base, Jackson drove Burt Hooton's first pitch, a fastball, on a low line into the right-field seats. When Jackson trotted into the dugout, Yankee teammates mobbed him, and

Billy Martin—who had tried to drop Jackson with a punch to the jaw in June—now patted him gleefully on his cheek.

In the fifth inning, again with a runner on base, Jackson jumped on Elias Sosa's first offering, another fastball, and hammered it on a hard line that traced again to the right-field stands. The stadium erupted. He trotted the bases with his shoulders back, his chin up. Again the players swarmed him in the dugout. Fans chanted for him to tip his hat.

By the time he strolled to the plate in the eighth, as memorable as any walk he ever made, the very air felt electrically charged. Were we witnessing one of the greatest performances in baseball history, a World Series performance for the ages, and in the House That Ruth Built? Yes, we were. Jackson stepped sharply into Charlie Hough's first pitch, a knuckleball that did not knuckle, and crushed it in the general direction of Queens.

The titanic blow, and the moment, inspired columnist Red Smith to pen a few rainbow lines reminiscent of his late friend, Grantland Rice, writing in the *New York Times*:

> Straight out from the plate the ball streaked, not toward the neighborly stands in right, but on a soaring arc toward the unoccupied bleachers in dead center . . . Up the white speck climbed, dwindling, diminishing, until it settled at least halfway up those empty stands, probably 450 feet away.

The Yanks won the game, 8–4, and with it the World Series. I can still hear Tom Lasorda, the losing Dodger manager, saying, "It was the greatest performance I ever saw in a World Series."

Now, I left the mound and moved across the outfield to Monument Park, where a Yankee tour guide was leading about twenty young visitors through that hallowed little patch of ground where old Yankee heroes have been enshrined in a kind of Bronx hagiography. The visitors stopped and stared as they entered the place. There in front of them, as stark as tombstones in a country churchyard, were four bronze plaques representing, in bas-relief, the cheery visages of Ruth, Gehrig, Huggins, and Mickey Mantle. Nine young boys from Yorktown, New York, were there to visit, and as they stood there looking at those old stone slabs, one of the boys, ten-year-old Chris Raiano, said what all of them were wondering at the moment.

"Are they all buried here?" Chris asked.

"No they are not," Deirdre Weldon, a mother of one of the boys, replied. "Only the memories are."

You can tear her down, brick by brick. You can haul her off to Montauk Point. But you cannot now, you cannot ever, steal her eternal ghosts away from here.

PETE HAMILL

That August morning in 1948, the newspapers were still full of the story: Babe Ruth was dead. The greatest home run hitter who ever lived had lost his painful battle with cancer. Flags flew at half-mast. Prayers were said in the churches and synagogues. At Sanew's candy store in our neighborhood in Brooklyn, my brother Tommy and I bought all seven daily newspapers, plus the *Brooklyn Eagle*, gazing in wonder at the black-bordered photographs of the man they called the Bambino. We cut out the stories, photographs, and cartoons and pasted them with mucilage into a scrapbook. We wanted to save every piece of the event. After all, this was history, and we hadn't witnessed much of it. Or so we thought. Tommy was eleven. I was thirteen.

The year before, we had seen baseball and history joined for the first time, when Jackie Robinson came to play for the Dodgers. With Robinson, we sensed that nothing would ever again be the same, and we were right. But the death of Babe Ruth wasn't about glorious beginnings or grace under pressure; it was the end of a story that was more myth than history, as remote and mysterious to us as the tales of Greek gods we read in the public library.

There was one difference: the body of this immortal would be laid out in the rotunda of Yankee Stadium. Neither Achilles nor Zeus ever said good-bye from the Bronx.

We read this in the newspaper, we wanted to leave immediately for that distant northern borough. It didn't matter that we had never been there before; in that infinitely more innocent New York, the young lived without a sense of menace. We hesitated because Babe Ruth was the ultimate Yankee. In Brooklyn, in the years after the war, this was no small thing. As adepts in the secular religion that worshiped at Ebbets Field, we sneered at the Giants and feared the Cardinals, but we hated the Yankees. They were arrogant. They were too perfect. They had beaten us in seven games the previous October in the World Series, in spite of Lavagetto's pinch hit in the ninth inning that broke up Bill Bevens' no-hitter, in spite of Al Gionfriddo's amazing catch of Joe DiMaggio's long drive. Yankee Stadium might have been the House That Ruth Built but to us it was the enemy camp.

So we debated the question with Talmudic intensity, and in the end, headed for the subway. After all, Ruth wasn't always a Yankee. In the second game of the 1916 World Series, he had pitched for the Boston Red Sox against the Dodgers and lasted fourteen great innings before the Red Sox won it, 2–1. If the Dodgers had to lose, at least they lost to Babe Ruth—as a pitcher! And hadn't the Babe, scorned by the Yankees, finished his career as a coach for the Dodgers in 1938? Of course. The papers kept insisting on another big point: Ruth wasn't just a Yankee; he was baseball. And so, in an example of what Catholic theologians called an "elastic conscience," we took the subway to say a farewell prayer for George Herman Ruth.

Almost a half century later, I don't remember what trains we took, and neither does my brother Tom. But I remember clearly coming around a corner in the Bronx and seeing Yankee Stadium for the first time. It was huge and clean and perfect, like a brand-new Cadillac compared to the rickety Model A of Ebbets Field. The day was hot. Vendors filled the streets, selling photographs and souvenirs of the Babe. And as we joined the huge line which hugged the wall of the stadium, we could smell loamy earth, the fresh, humid odor of outfield grass.

I tried to imagine what Babe Ruth must have looked like as he moved around on that grass, in the house that he built with his 42-ounce bat. There was no television then, and the newsreels only showed Ruth taking his gigantic swings and sending balls where they had never landed before. We never once saw him catch a ball. In all those photographs, we saw a heavy, pigeon-toed man. Surely he couldn't run like Robinson. Certainly he could not chase down a ball as well as Duke Snider, who had come up to the Dodgers in 1947 too. We didn't even think (standing in line, heady with the perfume of a summer ballpark, murmuring to each other lest Yankee fans discover our secret National League hearts) he could have fielded the position as well as Terry Moore of the Cardinals.

Still, he was Babe Ruth. And he was dead. So we stopped our own chatter, cut off our doubts, and waited on line among the Irishmen and the Italians, the Jews and the Latinos, the Blacks and the Germans, the mechanics and stockbrokers, the waitresses and welders and boys like us. We waited, that is, with the people of New York.

At last, we were a few feet away from the coffin. It was open to the summer air. And I remember the silence. It wasn't ordered. It wasn't even demanded. But there was a hush there in the shadows of the rotunda, and the hush made even two boys sense the finality of death. We arrived at the coffin and stared down at the face of the greatest home run hitter on the planet. His eyes were closed and he wore an expression of exhaustion. He skin was loose and powdery.

I whispered a Hail Mary and moved on. We lingered on the sidewalk for only a moment, gazing up at the looming perfect bulk of the stadium. On principle, we did not go inside. We did not look at home plate or the grass of the outfield. This was not our church. But just before we hurried home to Brooklyn, I was certain I could hear the crack of the bat and a huge deafening roar as Babe Ruth put another brick into the walls of his house.

*Editor's note: This piece was originally published in the book *Yankee Stadium: 75 Years of Drama, Glamor and Glory*, by Ray Robinson and Christopher Jennison (Viking, 1998) and appears here with the permission of the authors.

RAY ROBINSON

I have many memories of Yankee Stadium, but one that comes to mind is a brief encounter on a subway ride up to the Bronx many years ago. First, let me give you some history. I attended Columbia University, like my father before me. In 1940, the year before America's involvement in World War II, Dr. Kenneth Hechler, a young, energetic instructor of politics, introduced some quirky innovations in his class, presumably to keep his students awake. He invited a number of prominent figures of that era, literally a who's who in public affairs, to appear in person in the classroom at Morningside Heights. When these famous folks arrived they were pelted with questions by curious students.

Should a guest speaker be too busy to attend, Dr. Hechler broadcasted the lecture over speakerphone to his Government 21-22 class, enabling students to eavesdrop on Supreme Court justices, maverick *Emporia Gazette* editor William Allen White, Republican presidential candidate Wendell L. Willkie, and Communist party chieftain Earl Browder.

When the students arrived to class, they never knew who would wind up on the other end of a long-distance call.

One heavy hitter who appeared in person, not once but twice, was James Aloysius Farley. At the time, Farley—known to intimates as "Big Jim"—was head of the Democratic National Committee, postmaster general of the United States and President Franklin D. Roosevelt's former campaign manager. He helped guide FDR to two victories in his race for New York governor and two triumphs in his run for the presidency.

Farley was also a man of the diamond, that is to say a man of baseball, especially the Yankees.

Farley never met a baseball game that he didn't like. Born in Grassy Point, New York, thirty miles outside of New York City, in 1888, he grew up wanting to be a Yankees first baseman. He played semipro ball in Haverstraw, New York, before getting into local politics.

When the Yankees moved into their grand new ballpark in 1923, Farley immediately bought a season ticket. In April of that year, he was one of 74,000 fans who jammed into the new baseball palace to see Babe Ruth bang the Stadium's first home run and lead the Yankees to victory over the Red Sox. Farley remained on the precious season ticket list for the rest of his life, attending games whenever he was in New York. According to no less an authority than the late historian Arthur Schlesinger, Farley rarely missed an opener.

He was also in attendance on July 4, 1939 along with Mayor Fiorello LaGuardia, to hear Lou Gehrig deliver his touching valedictory.

I was a sad-eyed nineteen-year-old spectator that day at the Stadium, sitting in the faraway right-field bleachers, unlike Big Jim, who watched the proceedings from a box seat.

That same year, after Yankees owner Jacob Ruppert died, Farley, who had dreamed often that he might buy the club, put together a consortium of backers who shared his desire to own the Yankees. Not a rich man himself, Farley enlisted the help of FDR's former law partner Basil O'Connor, who was also a prominent money-raiser in the fight against infantile paralysis, a disease that FDR contracted in the 1920s.

When the negotiations fell through, Farley was distraught. Around the same time, his effort to become the Democratic nominee for president in 1940 also collapsed, as did his relationship with FDR.

But one constant in his life remained: the Yankees. And he never stopped showing up at the Stadium.

In his appearance at Dr. Hechler's class that spring morning in 1940, Farley delivered a chatty, "off the record" talk. When he finished his remarks, Farley suggested that each student be introduced to him.

My recollection is that I spent about three seconds in front of Big Jim. Dr. Hechler announced my name to him, Farley shook my hand, and then he greeted the next student. And so it went. Maybe thirty students passed through the ritual.

I never saw Farley again outside of seeing his picture in the newspapers, often when he was attending Yankees ballgames.

That was until some thirty years later, when I shared a subway car with him en route to Yankee Stadium.

Then in his early eighties, the ruddy-faced Farley sat across from me, a straw boater atop his bald head. A dark suit covered his broad-shouldered, ample 6-foot-2 frame. As our eyes met, he nodded at me and smiled.

"How are you today, Mr. Robinson?" he asked.

In a state of utter amazement at Farely's exercise in mnemonics, I returned his smile. Farley had known and met thousands of the most celebrated people in America and the world. Yet his mind, a multilayered index of names, faces, and places out of his colorful past, also had room in it to recall those eager Columbia students, including myself.

Perhaps the most amusing tale ever told about Farley's total recall was written by popular *Hearst* columnist Bugs Baer. Kiddingly, Baer challenged the notion that Farley was the ultimate master at matching names with faces.

"He's just a fraud," wrote Baer. "The way he gets the name is to keep shaking hands with the stranger, and slapping him on the back with his other hand. All the while he'd be telling the guy how glad he is to see him. Eventually, the bum's calling card would pop out of his vest, and Jim's got the guy's name!"

For a few moments on the subway, Farley and I exchanged comments about the state of the Yankees instead of the state of the Union. Then we each went on our way.

BOB COSTAS

To me Yankee Stadium means the original Yankee Stadium. I know the 1976 through 2008 version saw a lot of great moments and houses a lot of memories, but since I'm from a generation prior to that, at least in terms of remembering baseball, my earliest memories are of the classic Yankee Stadium where Mickey Mantle, Roger Maris, or for that matter, Bobby Murcer, played on exactly the same field with exactly the same dimensions as Ruth, Gehrig, and DiMaggio. That's what resonates most for me.

The first game I ever saw in person was the second-to-last day of the 1959 season. Saturday afternoon. It was one of those rare years, in that era, when the Yankees did not win the pennant. They finished third that year behind the White Sox and the Indians. I was seven years old. My father took me and my cousin.

My father was a huge baseball fan, very knowledgeable. His allegiances ran more towards the National League than the American, but there was that four-season window, 1958 to '61, when the Yankees were the only team in New York. Most members of my family were either Giant fans or Dodger fans, but when I first became conscious of baseball, the Yankees were the only New York team, so they became my team. The

Yankees televised a lot of games, even in that era. Mel Allen and Red Barber were in the booth along with the just-retired Phil Rizzuto. The games were on Channel 11 in black and white; I don't think the Yankees started broadcasting in color until 1966.

Anyway, they were playing the Orioles that day. My cousin, who was older than me, was a Giants fan and loved Willie Mays just as much as I loved Mantle. Since the Giants weren't involved, he insisted on wearing an Orioles cap, which infuriated me. I had a Yankee cap, and we were seated in the lower left-field stands—not the bleachers but the lower left-field stands, not far from the 402 sign that was just on the left-field side of the bullpen.

There wasn't that big of a crowd. My cousin and I had our gloves, like kids always did, and as the game moved along, we moved down closer and closer because we were convinced that a home run or a ground-rule double would soon land right in that area. We weren't just disappointed, we were amazed that none did. The Yankees lost the game, 7–2. I remember Johnny Blanchard hitting a home run. Mantle did not play, which was an enormous letdown.

We didn't keep score that day, but we bought souvenirs. I'll be the one millionth person to testify to this, but the thing you were struck by was the colors. Because your orientation to baseball, even if you were a very aware seven-year-old kid, was radio, black-and-white television, and black-and-white pictures in the newspaper.

And now you walk in and you're struck, not just the color, but by how arresting the colors are. The orange of the warning track, how emerald green the grass was, how pure white the batter's box and chalk lines and the bases were before the game started, the copper color of the façade. It was such an overwhelming place, the scale of it was enormous, and it was breathtaking, especially for a little kid.

Not to diminish the new Yankee Stadium, because many players and fans feel strongly about it, and it had great features like Monument Park, but it wasn't the old place. Not quite as awe-inspiring. The third baseball game I ever did on network television was in 1980. I was twenty-eight years old. The Yankees were playing the Tigers on the last Saturday of the regular season. The Tigers were bad then, but the previous night's game had been rained out, holding the Yankees' clinching number at one. There were a bunch of other games that day—one involved the Dodgers, and the other was the Phillies and Expos. These were supposed to be the featured games on NBC, and the Yankee game was a backup game in case of rain elsewhere. It did rain in Montreal, and the game there was delayed something like four hours.

Eventually, the Phillies won that night; I think Mike Schmidt hit a home run to clinch the division. So this combination of circumstances, a rainout, the Yankees stalled at one, and suddenly this game went out to the whole country.

And I'm sure nobody outside of St. Louis had any idea who I was. I'm doing the game with Bobby Valentine. The Yankees win the game. Reggie hits a home run into the upper deck, his forty-first and it ties Ben Ogilvie for the league lead. Goose Gossage comes in and saves the game, and they clinch the division. A memorable first time in the Yankee Stadium booth.

Subsequently, when I became part of the Game of Week team with Tony Kubek, we did many games at the Stadium. One happened to be Old Timers' Day and Mickey Mantle came into the booth for a few innings. I tried to be as professional as I could—that is, when I wasn't pinching myself. Later, I did a number of playoff and World Series games there, but even with the pennant and World Series on the line, I never heard the Stadium any louder than it was for Mickey Mantle Day in 1969. Mantle had retired prior to the season and this was the final send-off day. They retired his uniform. The place was full, which was remarkable because the capacity was huge back then and they didn't sell out often.

DiMaggio and Whitey Ford were part of the ceremony. Mickey's remarks were simple, humble, but in their own way eloquent and moving, and there was a sustained eight- to ten-minute ovation. I don't remember ever hearing a more appreciative reaction at a ball game.

(As told to Alex Belth)

ALLEN BARRA

My father took me to Yankee Stadium for the first time in 1961. It was a game scarcely anyone remembers – I do remember Arnold Hano mentioning it in, I think, the Willie Mays book he wrote in the *SPORT* magazine series, or perhaps it was the special Mickey Mantle–Willie Mays issue that *SPORT* magazine did in the spring of 1962. It was a charity game played between the Yankees and the San Francisco Giants, and it was Willie Mays's return to New York after three seasons.

I'll never forget my first look at Yankee Stadium: it seemed like the inside of New York City. And I'll never forget the crescendo that built up when Mays stepped out of the dugout and into the on-deck circle. Mantle, batting left-handed, hit a home run that day. (I could follow the arc of the ball perfectly as we were seated in a box seat on the third base line.) But Mays won the game with a single that drove in two runs.

One of the most vivid memories of my life was the afternoon of Monday, September 30, 1963, when my father came home from work—we were living in Old Bridge, New Jersey, and my father and all our neighbors commuted effortlessly to Manhattan—and held up two tickets for the opening game of the 1963 World Series. I never thought to ask how he got them, though I think he said something years later about it being a business friend he met at Toots Shor's saloon.

Nineteen sixty-three was one of the few years I didn't root for the Yankees; I was so excited about Sandy Koufax that I was ready to begin studying the Kabbalah. If you don't remember what the World Series was like back then in the days before prime time then it's hard to describe. It seemed to be on everywhere you went—TVs blaring out open windows, car radios at full blast, people walking the street and riding buses listening to transistor radios. I was told by my friend Jane Leavy that the Koufax Series—1963, 1965 and 1966—were the highest rated ever. I'm not surprised.

Our view was perfect, a box seat along the first-base line. In the first inning, Whitey Ford struck out the first two Dodgers and took a tapper back to the mound for the third out. I recall my father saying, "Well, Koufax is going to have to go some to top that." He did, of course, striking out the first five Yankees en route to a 5 2 victory.

I have one other strong recollection of Yankee history in the early sixties. My father knew a Westchester cop who was later indicted for taking huge amounts of money in the "Prince of the City" scandal. On New Year's Eve eve, he asked us if we wanted to join him and his son, a Fordham student, at the 1962 NFL Championship game between the Green Bay Packers and New York Giants. All I can recall is that it was the coldest day I could have imagined, and bundled up inside a hooded parka, I had my first shot of brandy from the cop's silver flask.

No, actually, as I write this a few other things come back to me: the way Green Bay's fullback Jim Taylor and Giants linebacker Sam Huff kicked, bit, and gouged each other and had to be separated after each play, and the way some of the punts would hit a wall of wind and flutter down to the concrete-like turf. The Packers' punter, Max McGee, I think it was, had one blocked for the Giants only touchdown.

Oddly, I did not feel that I was in the same stadium I had been in just two months earlier watching the Yankees and Giants play in the World Series. (My only memory of that game was how hyped everyone was about Mantle and Mays playing against each other.) I do not now recollect if I actually heard this or read about it afterwards: Someone yelled out when Mantle came out to bay, "Hey Mickey, we came to see who is the best, you or Willie. Now we're wondering who's the worst." Mantle popped up. As he walked back to the dugout, the man yelled, "Hey, Mantle, you win."

Bob Costas told me that he was also at the game and saw the same play from the same angle; we must have been seated right near each other.

For the life of me, I can't now recall whether you could see the Polo Grounds from the bleachers at Yankee Stadium or Yankee Stadium from the bleachers at the Polo Grounds.

In 1996, when the Yankees beat the Braves in the World Series, Allen St. John and I were out on the field. How this came about, I do not now recall—perhaps credentialed writers were allowed out on the field after games then. Someone in the dugout popped the first bottle of champagne, and the cork landed near us; Allen scooped it up and handed it to me. It now resides in a glass trophy case in my house.

DAVID ISRAEL

The first time I went to Yankee Stadium, Herb Score pitched for the Cleveland Indians and beat New York. It was 1956 and Score was twenty-three years old. By season's end, he would win twenty games and have a career record of 36-19. He was a star ascending as night descended on the career of Bob Feller. Lessons could be learned in the stands of Yankee Stadium, lessons about life, death, renewal. And promise unfulfilled. Not long thereafter, Herb Score would be hit in the face by a line drive. He would pitch six more seasons, winning nineteen games and losing twenty-seven.

I came of baseball age during that weird, brief interregnum between 1958 and 1962 when the Yankees were the only game in town. I had seen the Dodgers play once in Ebbets Field and the Giants once in the Polo Grounds. The Giants were my team. Willie Mays was my hero. The arguments were absurd. Mickey and the Duke didn't even belong in the conversation. But distance didn't make the heart grow fonder. The ardor faded. Another lesson learned. This time about abandonment. Sports, I would come to understand, are about transition. From offense to defense. From hope to disappointment. From one season to another. Turn, turn, turn. The Byrds provide the music and the lyrics.

I was a kid sitting with his father in the mezzanine—just to the first base side of home plate—on July 13, 1960, when Willie Mays, Eddie Matthews, and Stan Musial hit home runs to lead the National League to a 6–0 victory in the All-Star Game. But what I remember most vividly, what I recall as if it just happened yesterday, is Ted Williams singling down the right-field line in his final All-Star at-bat. A few months later, the Kid bid the Hub adieu with a home run and downcast eyes. He never looked up, he never tipped his cap, because, John Updike wrote, "Gods do not answer letters." But on this bright sunny day in New York, Ted Williams stopped at first base, bounced on his toes, waited for Brooks Robinson to replace him as a pinch runner, looked up at the towering grandstand— three decks high, copper façade turned green by the scientific phenomenon of oxidation (something else I learned by sitting in the stands of Yankee Stadium)—and soaked it all in. I saw Ted Williams swing a baseball bat just once, but in time I would come to understand that on July 13, 1960, in Yankee Stadium I had actually seen something done perfectly.

Later, I would cover the World Series at Yankee Stadium. I would sit in the same press box as Red Smith and Jim Murray. I would see Reggie Jackson hit three home runs in one game, suppress the urge to cheer diving stops by cantankerous Graig Nettles, admire the skill of Catfish Hunter, the cunning of Ron Guidry, the power of Goose Gossage (a Goose and a Catfish on the same pitching staff; almost as good as a Catfish, a Blue Moon, and a Vida on one staff), and the tenacity of Thurman Munson.

I spent some of the best days of my wasted youth at Yankee Stadium, even though I hated the Yankees.

Partly, that is because deep down, as a child and a young man, I respected the Yankees.

Mostly, though, that is because Yankee Stadium had another home team. My New York Football Giants.

It was the House That Ruth Built, but for me Gifford, Conerly, Tittle, Rote, Brown, Barnes, Lynch, Patton, Huff, Webb, Robustelli, Modzewlewski, Chandler, Summerall, Webster, Morrison, and Shofner made it a home.

From September 1961 through December 1968, I never missed a Giants home game. My father got season tickets when they played in the Polo Grounds and moved with them to Yankee Stadium. He saw the Greatest Game Ever Played in 1958, and when I was old enough to appreciate what was going on, I became his partner every Sunday. Our seats were above the auxiliary scoreboard in right field. It was a lousy place to watch a baseball game, but damn near perfect for football. Section 53, Row 5, Seat 5. We were behind the visitors' bench, between the 35- and 40-yard lines.

Shirtsleeves in September; rain gear in November; parkas, long johns, ear muffs, and gloves in December. Turn, turn, turn.

The Giants played for championships the first three seasons, and suffered ingloriously the next five. Life is change. Nothing lasts forever.

We would drive into the Bronx from Jersey, find a parking space on the street, stop by the sandlot game at Macombs Dam Park, and then head up the hill to the Jerome Cafeteria, where we ate lunch.

I was in the Jerome eating an egg salad sandwich, listening to the transistor radio, just a little while before the Giants played the St. Louis Cardinals on November 24, 1963, when I heard Lee Harvey Oswald had been shot. We went to the game that Sunday. Life goes on. Years later, Pete Rozelle became my friend. But I never asked him if he regretted not canceling the NFL's games the weekend JFK was shot.

I was in my seat in the right-field bleachers for the 1962 championship game against Vince Lombardi's Green Bay Packers. It was the coldest I've ever been, probably the most uncomfortable I've ever been. I was eleven years old and I risked frostbite. But I wouldn't have had it any other way. Well, almost. I wish the Giants had won. I remember the cold. And I remember snapshots of the game. Sam Huff tangling with Jim Taylor. Jerry Kramer, who later became a friend and let my wife try on his Super Bowl ring, playing every play at guard and kicking the three field goals that won the game, 16–7, for Green Bay because Paul Hornung was hurt. But mostly I remember the cold.

I was in the same seat another day, a warmer, better, more meaningful day. I'm not sure who the Giants played that day—maybe Philadelphia—and I'm not sure what the score was or who won. But I remember the shadows of the grandstand creeping across the field and I remember a play, one play, a pass thrown by Y. A. Tittle, called Pete's Special. It was a gadget play and it was named for one of the Petes who worked in the Giants clubhouse—either Sheehy or Previte, I can't remember which—who suggested it to coach Allie Sherman. The Giants spread the field with extra wide receivers borrowed from their defense, the safety Jim Patton and the cornerback Erich Barnes. They went long, and Tittle hit Barnes for a touchdown. The crowd went crazy. Something new. Something different. And it worked. But what I remember most is the celebration on the field. No one danced. No one spiked the ball. No one pulled out a pen or shadowboxed the goal post. But Jimmy Patton, a white man from Ole Miss, ran over and hugged Erich Barnes, a black man from Purdue, in the end zone. This was in 1961 or 1962. This was the age of Bull Connor and governors standing in schoolhouse doors. This was before Selma, before Schwerner,

Chaney, and Goodman. This was before the Civil Rights Act, the Voting Rights Act, before Martin Luther King, Jr., stood on the steps of the Lincoln Monument and let the dream ring out.

Jimmy Patton hugged Erich Barnes in the shadow of the Yankee Stadium grandstand.

I learned a lesson that day. Maybe the most important lesson I ever learned in my life.

Turn. Turn. Turn.

VIC ZIEGEL

Many many years ago, as usual, the Yankees PR person, Bob Fishel, asked me to speak to a group of high school sports editors. They put us in the lower left-field stands, well before a day game. This was the year Mailer and Breslin were running for mayor and president of the city council. My friend, Joe Flaherty, who would later collect their campaign adventures into a marvelous book, *Managing Mailer*, provided me with all the campaign buttons.

The one I wore to the stadium was END THE BULLSHIT. I thought the kids would enjoy it. What I wasn't told, until later, was that they were predominantly from the suburbs. The swanky suburbs. So I gave my little speech, answered a bunch of questions, and it was all was going smoothly. Until one young man asked what the button meant.

I smiled, and responded, "That's a Mailer-Breslin campaign button. They're running for..."

But I was cut off by long, loud boos. Surprised, I mumbled the rest of my sentence. I blamed it on the Westchester in their souls. Made me long for those predictable days when kids used to ask who was better, Mays or Mantle.

MAURY ALLEN

This was in 1972 in the old Yankee Stadium, the one where Ruth, Gehrig, DiMaggio, and Mantle had played, long before the 1974–75 refurbishing and a dream location across from the House That Steinbrenner Built for 2009.

I walked on that green grass again as I had for a dozen years or so as a sportswriter, looked out at those monuments, examined that façade above the third deck, and waited for my pitching pal.

Fritz Peterson, the left-handed anchor of the bad Yankee pitching staff of the late 1960s and early 1970s, was on the field now, a smile on his face as always, his baseball cap tipped back, his eyes wide with glee and amusement.

"I got another tugboat postcard," he said, with that wry smile. "I put it in his locker."

Peterson had a habit of collecting postcards of big boats or even bigger women and dropping them off in the locker of Thurman Munson, the best Bronx Bomber catcher since Yogi. It irritated the surly Munson to no end.

Sparky Lyle, another laughing teammate, had once described Munson as not really moody.

"Moody is when you can smile some of the time," Lyle said of his unfortunate batterymate, later to lose his life in a 1979 plane crash.

We chatted a while about Peterson's next start in another strong season (17–15 in 1972 after 20 wins in 1970) and then I asked him if he was available on the next Yankees off-day for a barbecue at my suburban home.

"Sure," he said. "Can I bring Kekich?"

He had become pals with another Yankee lefty, Mike Kekich and the two couples, Fritz and Marilyn Peterson, Mike and Suzanne Kekich, had spent a lot of time together.

The four of them arrived at my home on a beautiful summer night. My wife Janet had gone all out with her best cooking, our best dishes, and a beer-filled refrigerator. A good time was had by all.

Soon, the information was out. Peterson and Kekich had arranged that night to swap wives, kids, cars, dogs, houses, and hearts.

Marilyn and Mike never lasted as a couple. Fritz and Suzanne are going on some thirty-five years together.

Some people will always remember the giant home runs at the Stadium hit by Mickey Mantle or the clutch World Series shots by Yogi Berra or the brilliance of Whitey Ford on the mound and Elston Howard behind the plate.

Me? I just remember standing on that famous green grass and simply asking Fritz Peterson to join us for a barbecue. Who knew what evil lurked behind that question?

GEORGE KIMBALL

There are things you learned about the old Yankee Stadium once it became your place of work that never would have occurred to you as a kid going to watch a game there. Making your way from the visiting to the home-team dugout, or to the pressroom where they fed us and the adjacent quarters where we wrote our stories after games, involved negotiating an elaborate system of labyrinthine tunnels that could have been a large-scale Skinner box. A dim-witted scribe could spend hours trying to find his way around down there, but once he did figure it out, he'd be rewarded with supper, or maybe a beer after the game.

And since we only made two or three trips a year to New York, we were always making wrong turns, ones that inevitably brought us face-to-face with one of New York's finest on a security detail. Some of the cops had been drawing this plum assignment for years. Others, newer to the job, couldn't tell you how to get from A to B any better than another sportswriter could. They should have handed out road maps with the press credentials.

But the overriding memory of all those hours spent wandering around beneath the House That Ruth Built remains the smell.

If you grew up in suburbia, it wouldn't have meant much to you at all, but if you'd spent much time in a big-city tenement or in the stockroom of a grocery store or ever wandered beneath street level in a restaurant that abuts a subway line, the permeating odor of Decon, the rat poison, would have been familiar.

My friend, John Schulian, must have recognized that smell too, because at some point in the late 1970s, he came up with a description of Billy Martin so apt that it should have been chiseled on Billy's gravestone:

A rat studying to be a mouse.

The funny part of it was that, while Martin had carefully cultivated an image of a guy ready to fight at the drop of a hat, he wasn't actually very good at it. If you look at the fights he won, they were usually against marshmallow salesmen or mental cripples (Jimmy Piersall was just months away from the loony bin when Martin beat him up under the stands at Fenway in 1952) or a guy who was even drunker than he was (Dave Boswell at the Lindell AC in 1969). Sometimes he'd gain the advantage with a well-timed sucker punch, and sometimes he'd just *think* he had the advantage, as was the case in St. Louis in 1953, when he picked a fight with a short guy wearing glasses. (The guy, Clint "Scrap-Iron" Courtney, turned out to run against stereotype.)

If you watched him carefully over the years, he was cautious to pick his spots. When Martin went at it with somebody bigger or tougher than he was, it was usually in a setting where he knew it would get broken up right away. In fair fights—and there weren't many of them—he almost always got his ass kicked. (See: Martin vs. Ed Whitson at the Cross Keys Inn, Baltimore, 1985.)

I'd been at Yankee Stadium the night Thad Tillotson bounced a pitch off Joe Foy's helmet in 1967. "Watch this," I told my then-wife when Tillotson came to bat a couple of innings later. Sure enough, Jim Lonborg drilled him in the back, both benches emptied, and when they finally pulled them apart, there were Joe Pepitone and Rico Petrocelli rolling around in the dirt.

I was also at Fenway Park the day in 1973 when Stick Michael missed a bunt on a suicide squeeze. With Thurman Munson barreling in from third toward Carlton Fisk, whom he didn't like much anyway, the result was somewhat predictable. Both benches emptied after the collision, and even as they dragged Munson away, Fisk and Michael were going at it. Boston lefty Bill "Spaceman" Lee said the whole thing looked like a bunch of hookers swinging their purses at each other.

Everyone save Thurman Munson thought that was pretty funny.

So, by the time Billy Martin came back to manage his old team, Red Sox–Yankee rhubarbs were nothing new. Their history long predated the return of Number One. I'd seen them start for good reasons and for bad reasons, and sometimes they'd started just because they were the Yankees and Red Sox.

So, when another one broke out on May 20, 1976, I wasn't surprised. You could see this one coming a mile down the road. It was like watching a fight develop in slow motion.

Lee had a 1–0 lead with two out in the bottom of the sixth. Lou Piniella, at second, represented the tying run; Graig Nettles was on first. With the count 2–1 on Otto Velez, Spaceman threw a sinker on the outside of the plate, and Velez stroked it into the opposite field. It was hit so hard that when Dwight Evans grabbed it on one hop, it briefly crossed my mind that he might even have a play on Nettles at *second*. That's when I looked down and saw Piniella rounding third, and he didn't seem to be slowing down.

Evans may have had the best arm in the American League back then, and not even a *good* base runner would have challenged him in this situation, but Piniella was, at this point, committed and kept on coming. Evans threw in one fluid motion, a strike to the plate, and had him by at least ten feet. If it had somehow been a closer play, maybe what happened next wouldn't have happened at all, but now it was inevitable.

Out by a mile, Piniella's only chance was to run right over Fisk, barreling into him so hard that he might dislodge the ball. Fisk, aware of this, was determined to make the experience painful enough that Lou would think twice before he ever tried it again.

As tags go, it *was* pretty aggressive. Fisk may even have tried to tag him in the nuts—and with his fist, not his glove, holding the ball. Naturally, Lou came up swinging, and in what seemed barely an instant, there were fifty or sixty guys in uniform going at it in the middle of the infield.

Or that's the way it seemed. Actually, some of them took a bit longer getting there than others. Traditional baseball protocol in these situations calls for the occupants of both bullpens, even the ones intent on serving as peacemakers, to make a mad dash all the way to the infield, where they are to then grab one of their opposite numbers and wrestle for a while until the smoke clears.

Logic would suggest that it would be a lot simpler to just pair off out in the bullpen, particularly since, in its new configuration, Yankee Stadium's bullpens shared a common gate.

So, when the fight started, everybody from both bullpens jumped up simultaneously to race in to where the action was. Tom House, then a Boston reliever, told me that when he got to the gate, Catfish Hunter was gallantly holding it open for him.

"See ya in there, kid," said Catfish as House trotted past.

Fisk and Piniella were rolling around on the ground following the collision when Lee, who'd been backing up the plate on the play, spotted Velez trying to be third man in. The first guy to hit Lee was actually Mickey Rivers, who must have been taking boxing lessons from Billy Martin. Mick was running up and down behind the scrum, looking like a guy playing Whack-A-Mole as he lashed out at the back of every Boston cap he could spot. (Somebody watching on television later told me that Ken Harrelson, in his blow-by-blow call on a Boston station, said "Rivers is just basically just running around sucker-punching *everybody!*")

The next thing I saw was Nettles grabbing Spaceman from behind, seemingly lifting him over his head, and body-slamming him. I don't know for a fact that he was *trying* to throw Lee on his left shoulder, but that's how he landed. (Nettles claimed later that he was just trying to drag Lee off Velez, since Rivers' punch hadn't done the job.)

Lee was 6-foot-3 and 210 pounds, almost the exact dimensions of Muhammad Ali, but truth be told, he couldn't fight any better than Billy Martin could, even though he did have an impressive one-punch KO on his résumé.

That had occurred in a winter league game down in Mayaguez, Puerto Rico, several years earlier. When Eliseo Rodriguez charged the mound, Lee reflexively stuck his hand out in self-defense and, to his own surprise, knocked Rodriguez cold. Only when he read the next morning's papers did he realize that he'd knocked out the island's former Golden Gloves light-heavyweight champion.

The return bout took place in Caguas a week later. Rodriguez and two of his relatives were waiting when Spaceman got off the team bus. They beat him up and rammed his face into a light pole for good measure.

"I did get a nice new set of teeth out of the deal," said Spaceman.

With Lee now apparently out of commission, Fisk and Piniella separated and Rivers dragged away by several Yankees, things seemed to calm down in a hurry. That's when Lee made the mistake of getting up.

In his college days at USC, Bill had played summer ball for the Alaska Goldpanners with Nettles' brother. Until a few moments earlier, he had considered Graig a friend. Now, he was screaming incomprehensibly as he staggered toward the New York third baseman.

"I think," Lee said later, "it might have been the word 'asshole' that set him off."

In Nettles' defense, what he probably saw was just a crazy man charging at him. In any case, when Lee got close enough, Nettles cut loose with a right cross, and when Lee tried to block it with his left, he discovered that he couldn't lift his arm above his waist. The punch caught Spaceman flush in the face and dropped him in his tracks.

A few months later, Ali and Ken Norton fought in almost exactly the same spot, and in fifteen rounds neither one of them landed a punch as hard as that one.

Oddly, I don't remember Billy Martin throwing a single punch in that brawl. Maybe he found Don Zimmer and the two of them sat it out.

Once order was restored, both Nettles and Lee were ejected. (Neither Fisk nor Piniella were.) In Lee's case, it was somewhat moot. Before the Red Sox finished batting in the next inning, he was on his way to the hospital.

He would later describe the episode by saying "I was attacked by Billy Martin's brownshirts."

There was clearly no love lost between the dope-smoking Spaceman and the whiskey-swilling Fiery Genius. There were unconfirmed rumors, before and since, that Martin had personally placed a bounty on Lee, but there were enough Yankees players who intensely disliked Lee that they probably didn't need any encouragement from Billy Martin.

Obviously, the fight hadn't been started just to get at him, said Lee, "but once it did start, it sure seemed like there were a lot of guys in pinstripes trying to find me."

It might be noted here that, going into that game, Lee ranked as the number three Yankee-killer of all time, with a lifetime percentage against the Bronx Bombers bettered only by those of Babe Ruth and Dickie Kerr. Ruth, of course, had stopped pitching even before Harry Frazee sold his contract to Colonel Ruppert, and Kerr, pointed out Lee, may have accomplished the greatest pitching feat of all time—winning two games in the 1919 World Series with five guys playing behind him who were trying to lose.

Bill Lee's career didn't end that night, but it's fair to say he was never the same pitcher again. He had won seventeen games in each of the previous three years, but he never won as many in a season again. He had torn ligaments and a separated left shoulder, and nearly two months would go by before he pitched again. Between 1973 and 1975 Lee had thrown fifty-one complete games. In 1976 he would throw just one.

Nobody knew this that night at that ballpark, of course. All we knew was that Lee had been taken away in an ambulance, but when the team bus pulled up in front of the New York Sheraton an hour and a half after the last out, there was Spaceman, waiting in the lobby.

Since I was then writing for a weekly and didn't face a post-game deadline, Lee and I had earlier made plans to terrorize a saloon or two in Greenwich Village that night, and now, with his arm and a sling and sporting a black eye, he was determined to keep the appointment.

"Come on," he said. "We're still going to the Lion's Head, aren't we?"

Stan Williams, the Red Sox's pitching coach, had other ideas. "Come on, big boy," he said to Lee as he grabbed his good arm. "No curfew for you tonight."

So, with Stanley as our tour guide, we went bouncing on the Upper East Side. I vaguely remember visiting a gin mill with a hospital motif—the ER? the Recovery Room?—where the waitresses were all dressed like nurses, or dressed like nurses wearing white miniskirts, anyway.

Either the sight of a bona fide patient had scared all the nurses away or we'd moved on to another joint. Thirty-three years later, all I can swear to is that, a bit after 3 AM, we were the last three customers in the bar, and Lee had been chasing shots of VO with the Demerol they'd given him in the real hospital, or maybe it was the other way around, but anyway, just then the saloon door swings open and who comes walking in but—think about the odds of this for a moment—Lou Piniella, all by himself.

As soon as he saw us he was all over Lee like a long-lost brother: "Gee, Bill, I'm so sorry. If I'd ever known this was going to happen . . ." I think tears may even have welled up in his eyes. And, of course, he bought us all a drink, and then another one.

The sun was coming up by the time we left, Sweet Lou in one direction, and Bill, Stan, and I back to the hotel. In the cab, I remarked to Lee that Piniella was a pretty nice guy after all, and that he *had* seemed properly contrite over the outcome of the affair he'd initiated at home plate that night.

"What *else* was he going to say?" Spaceman sighed wearily. "There were three of us and one of him."

Out on an early morning foraging run, a solitary rat darted across the sidewalk. We all saw him, but nobody said a word.

LEIGH MONTVILLE

I was in the big time now, covering the 1977 World Series for the *Boston Globe*. I was thirty-four years old. I had covered the first two games in Yankee Stadium, the next three in Los Angeles, and was back in New York for Game 6.

I went to some hotel room to pick up my credentials on the afternoon of the game, and whoever was in charge gave me all of the credentials for the *Globe*. Opening the envelope, I immediately realized that whoever was in charge had made a mistake: there were two extra credentials in the pile.

A moral dilemma also was enclosed. I was a journalist, an adult, a member of a respected and ethical profession. (Return the credentials!) I also had grown up in nearby New Haven, Connecticut, hanging out with the same bunch of guys forever, our group called "The Garden Street Athletic Club." We had spent our lifetimes talking about sports, baseball, had made assorted trips to the Stadium starting back when we were in the Boy Scouts. (Call the boys! Now!)

I, of course, called the boys.

Charlie Costanzo, now a lawyer, came down from Connecticut. Ray-Ray, now a school administrator, came up from Philadelphia. We met outside the Stadium, and I gave them the credentials, which included full access to the field and locker rooms, and told them to please be cool. My job hung in the balance if they did something weird.

"No autographs," I said. "No talking with the players. Just be flies on the wall. Stay out of everyone's way. Have a good time."

All went well before the game. We hung out on the field, watched batting practice, even spotted Sal Trotta, one of our guys from Garden Street, in the crowd. ("I get the greatest seats ever for Game 6. I'm so proud of myself . . . then I look out and you guys ARE ON THE FIELD!") We ate dinner in the press-room. We watched the game from the press section.

What could be better?

Oh, yes, Reggie Jackson hit three home runs. The Yankees won the Series.

I told the boys again to stay out of trouble, wished them well on their trips home, plunged into the mob of reporters around the celebrating Bronx Bombers, found a few usable quotes, went back to the pressroom, and wrote yet another Pulitzer Prize account of what I had seen. The deadlines were harsh, after midnight, so the Pulitzer Prize account was written with great haste.

I packed up my typewriter, put on my coat, and decided to stop, one last time, in the Yankee clubhouse before I left. You never know. I would have to write some kind of follow-up story the next day.

The clubhouse was empty of players . . . except for Reggie Jackson. He was getting dressed at his locker, end of the greatest night of his career, still talking. He was well beyond the descriptions of the three homers, talking now about growing up in Baltimore, about his father, who was a tailor, talking about anything.

Talking to Ray-Ray.

Charlie Costanzo was sitting on a couch in the locker room, bored by now, wanting to go home. Reggie and Ray-Ray were by themselves. Alone. I'm not sure if Reggie thought he was talking to some famous writer from some famous place. I'm not sure if Ray-Ray thought he was some famous writer from some famous place. They seemed to get along. That was how one of the most famous nights in Yankee Stadium ended. Ray-Ray and Reggie.

Me, hoping that I wouldn't get fired.

TOM BOSWELL

My first visit to Yankee Stadium was in 1968. A college baseball teammate, who'd grown up in New York as a Yankee fan and Mickey Mantle worshipper, took me to the shrine. It was the only time I ever saw the original House That Ruth Built before the huge 1970s remodeling. The cathedral, severe and gray on the exterior but soaring and rimmed all around with white façade on the inside, was even more magnificent than I had imagined from a hundred games on black-and-white TV in my childhood.

The Yanks were lousy that year, so the afternoon crowd was small and the ushers let us into the box seats during batting practice. I've forgotten the game but still remember Reggie Jackson's pre-game throws from right field to third base. Every throw was full bore, on a line, never more than head-high, on one hop to third. His windup wasted time, but was perfect to attract attention and style points. And his green-yellow-and-white A's uniform seemed to make him glow.

Eight years later, I wrote in the *Washington Post* that Reggie was very smart, but loved his own voice so much that, "If he talked about the Bill of Rights long enough, you'd want to repeal it." Reggie came up to me in the clubhouse, pointed to the line, tapped his finger on the paper and said, "So true. So true."

* * *

Ray "Rabbit" Miller, pitching coach and manager for various teams, spent ten years in the minors, but never had a big league game. Yankee Stadium was his symbol that he'd made the major leagues even if he'd done it though a back door. Sometimes, if his team was in New York for a night game, he would come to the Stadium long before anyone else. In the early afternoon, the empty park looks so blue, so big that, in some ways, it's more impressive than when it's full. "I just sit in the dugout," Miller told me, "listening to the sounds that aren't there."

* * *

Soon after Roger Clemens came to the Yankees, Mike Flanagan, then in the Orioles' front office, asked the Rocket to allow his wife to do a plaster cast of his hands to be turned into a sculpture that she would sell at an auction for charity. Many stars did this for her good cause, and she would present the player with an extra sculpture of his hands in appreciation. On a Friday, Clemens blew her off. Saturday, same thing, but with a lame excuse about how he couldn't do it because "my hands are insured." On Sunday, Flanagan, a former Cy Young winner, told manager Joe Torre the problem. Torre had been trying to figure out how to get Clemens to understand the late '90s Yanks' code of personal behavior exemplified by Derek Jeter, Mariano Rivera, and Bernie Williams. He wanted to get him in line as a person, not as a player. Joe saw his chance. "Clemens!" yelled Torre across the Yankee clubhouse, "get your insured hands and your insured ass in my office right now!" Clemens came hustling like a little boy. And he did the plaster casts.

* * *

When Billy Martin managed the Yanks, his old buddies Yogi Berra and Whitey Ford were often in the clubhouse, either as coaches or special instructors, or just because they seemed to belong there. Yogi always mooched Whitey's personal products—toothpaste, soap, shaving cream. Whitey would bitch. Yogi kept doing it. Ford decided to get revenge. Whitey filled his deodorant stick with liquid glue. The whole Yankee clubhouse watched Yogi out of the corner of their eyes as he headed to the showers with the stolen glue deodorant. A few minutes later, Yogi comes back, arms stuck to his sides, walking like a penguin. The locker room erupted.

Thurman Munson liked to invite his grossest, orneriest-looking friend from his boyhood days, a huge fat guy named "Boot," to come to the Stadium to heckle visiting Red Sox players from a first-row box seat that Munson bought for him. In the Yankee clubhouse before one game, Munson said, "Boot, show 'em the trick." Boot put a firecracker between his front teeth, rocked his head back, lit it, and let it explode while he was holding it between his lips. "Call the Red Sox any name you want to call 'em," said Munson, loudly. "They're not going to mess with a three-hundred-pound guy who sets off firecrackers in his mouth."

When Martin returned to the Stadium as A's manager in 1980, he was unhappy—with me. I'd written a national magazine story saying his pitchers cheated. The American League office sent photographers to try to catch them scuffing, greasing, or spitting for their illegal pitches. In his office, Martin got inches from my face and yelled, several times, "You got a lot of guts coming in here." I was thirty-two. He was fifty-two and an alcoholic. Players told me that, as he'd gotten older, he turned into a sucker punch artist. If you flinched, he'd say he beat you to the punch. If you opened your mouth, he'd hit you in the jaw, then say you insulted him. Maybe it was strategy. Maybe I was paralyzed. I didn't move or speak. We were "separated." I survived.

* * *

In the winter of 2007–08, my wife and I went to the Kiku chrysanthemum festival at the New York Botanical Gardens. The subway went by, and above, both versions of Yankee Stadium—the old Big Ballpark and the new park under construction across the street. "There's Yankee Stadium," I said. She'd never seen it. "Oh," she said, surprised, "it's actually kind of pretty."

Before the '08 All-Star game, owner George M. Steinbrenner III, the symbol of baseball's age of free-agent financial excess since 1976, was driven in a golf cart to the pitcher's mound to receive the cheers of the crowd. Those fans well understood that this moment marked the end of old Boss's active direction of the Yanks, as his sons took control of operations. For me, that All-Star moment also completed two interconnected pieces of American history—one baseball, the other economic.

The Yankees were always the team of Wall Street, but never more so than in the greedy era of the Bronx Zoo under Steinbrenner. No bonus was too high, no leverage was too excessive, no method of performance enhancement—by steroid or derivative—was too risky, whether it was used in the Bronx or down in lower Manhattan.

By elegant coincidence, the original House That Ruth Built had a near-gut renovation for two years before the 1976 season. Not long after the Boss took control of the Yanks in 1973, arriving with all his bucks, a radically altered and not-quite-so-magnificent version of the Stadium was reopened to house his team. Then, the very year that the Boss left center stage, the park that held his Zoo disappeared, too.

Within months of that All-Star night when George III symbolically abdicated, the old Stadium was torn down. Who knew that, as Steinbrenner said his "good-bye," the foundations of Wall Street itself were already irrevocably cracked and that, as the Yankee season wound down, all five major investment banks would crumble into ruin or irrelevance in the Crash of '08—a wrecking ball awaited both.

*   *   *

In the final American League Championship Series game of 2004, Johnny Damon's second home run went straight over my head in the right-field press box, giving Boston an 8–1 lead. I immediately thought of my father-in-law, Sheik Karelis, born in 1920, a lifelong New Englander and much more than just a Red Sox fan. The best pitcher ever at the University of New Hampshire, Sheik signed with the Red Sox after several years in the navy in World War II. He got as far as Triple-A but never made it to Fenway Park, except in his heart. Every summer, my family would hear Sheik and his buddies in Haverhill, Massachusetts, relive their latest Red Sox agonies and Yankee horrors. On my cell phone, with the crowd silent, I could hear the eighty-four-year-old Sheik, who'd been born after the last Red Sox world title, yelling, "Boz, the Red Sox have exploded! New England is going crazy. My phone is ringing off the hook." I congratulated him, but he stopped me cold. "Let's see if they can hold this lead."

As we sat side-by-side in the auxiliary press box at some long-forgotten big ball game in the Big Ballpark in the '00s, Roger Angell, then past eighty, dean of American letters, stepson of E. B. White, author of *The Summer Game*, and fiction editor of *The New Yorker* for decades, whispered in my ear, "Lean forward, just a little bit, so I can hit that jerk who won't shut up with a spitball."

"Who is he anyway?" said Angell, rolling up a small paper wad.

"He's a nationally famous TV personality," I said.

"Oh," said Roger. "Well, I think I can get him right in the ear."

Using me as a shield, Angell threw sidearm behind my back and hit his target in the shoulder. But Mr. TV didn't notice, just kept pontificating. For several innings, he had been standing in the press box aisle, talking loudly with two sycophants, but never about the game in progress.

"Do it again," said Angell, as he fired another pellet. Other reporters noticed, but kept stone-faced. "Unbelievable," muttered Angell after an inning of fusillades failed to silence the inanities. "He's like a force of nature."

Angell upped his ante. Changing his voice, he'd lean behind me and yell, "Shut up," then jerk his head back. A minute later, "Watch the game." Then, "Quiet."

After two innings, the celebrity and entourage departed, pretending that undetected insurgents hadn't really driven them out. The aux box rustled its approval, no words, just nods of appreciation for a bench-jockeying job well done.

"That's better," said John Updike's editor. "Now we can enjoy the game." Angell looked happy as the devil.

ED RANDALL

The Stadium cast a long and continuing shadow on my life even though I didn't grow up a Yankees fan. I went to grammar and high school for twelve years in the same building at All Hallows just three blocks away and took the subway behind the center-field fence. I threw snowballs from the platform near pedestrians below while waiting for the northbound train. I saw my first game there and have very vague memories of being fascinated by the TV cameras in the outdoor photo box.

I recall standing near a ramp leading to the box seats as a child when a door swung open and there stood Johnny Blanchard in all his Yankee pinstriped splendor and his shiny black spikes that clicked when he took a step. It was breathtaking. Later, ironically, Johnny Blanchard, a fellow prostate cancer survivor, sat on the Advisory Board of my charity, Ed Randall's Bat for the Cure.

Back then, patrons in the lower level—which we could rarely afford—exited the park by *walking on the field!* Imagine slowly making your way along the warning track up the left-field line, turning right past the visiting bullpen and auxiliary scoreboard and then, the best part, past the monuments. More than once did I walk out onto River Avenue through the Yankee bullpen where countless home runs came to rest and where everyone from Joe Page onward warmed up. Somehow, even then I knew the importance of what I was experiencing.

That ritual made me want to do one thing: genuflect.

I pitched on weekends at Babe Ruth Field, obliterated to make way for the new stadium. I also threw at Macombs Dam Park, bordering the left-field line. You couldn't think about the fact that you could stand on the mound, turn slightly to your right, and throw a baseball and hit the Stadium wall. Then again, how do you ignore Yankee Stadium? Many years later, in a corporate outing, I pitched in Yankee Stadium, lined a single through the shortstop hole, and had a large bucket of ice water dumped on me by Rusty Staub and Jay Johnstone.

I was playing intramural softball freshman year in high school the day of the Yankees home opener in '67. All afternoon, it was strangely quiet inside. Then, late in the game, there was one tremendous roar. Elston Howard had broken up the no-hit bid of Boston's rookie lefty, Billy Rohr.

The September before, I was running on the track on a miserable, drizzly day. As Robert Palmer sang many years later in "Addicted to Love": "The lights are on and no one's home" as the Yankees played a midweek day game against Chicago. There was no noise as the game was played, none. How could there be? Only 413 were in the House That Ruth Built, capacity in excess of 62,000. It was the game that helped get Red Barber fired.

When I took driver's ed in the spring of my senior year in high school, Mr. Zaretsky had us learn how to shift gears and back up on what then was the flat parking lots across from first base, long before there was a multi-tiered lot and a really, really tall bat.

For two seasons, I sold hot dogs in a concession stand there and *still have* my badge from Canteen Corporation! I did it for the Giants, not the Yankees.

You see, I would get fired if I worked baseball because *I know* all I would do is watch the game and move very little product. In fact, in 1972, I showed up just one time, to work a night game against the White Sox. It was the night I first saw a young, hard-throwing pitcher named Goose Gossage. No earnings that night.

I was behind the counter in the bleachers—you can't imagine the dampness on your feet out there—listening on my transistor radio as Steve Blass of the Pirates completed a comeback from three-games-to-one-down to beat Baltimore in '71 (bet I was the only one in the house that day doing that). To this day, every time I think of Steve Blass or talk to him, I think of the bleachers in Yankee Stadium.

I was the host of home-game pre- and post-shows on Sports-Channel in 1988. In May, after Mickey Mantle left the booth after completing six innings of color commentary, I replaced him and did the final three innings of play-by-play. The adrenalin rush of sitting in his chair and looking out and seeing that subway station made me broadcast at approximately the same speed Secretariat raced Belmont.

I was there for the last game in '73, the first game in '76, for Whitey's last home start, a 14–0 loss to Palmer and the Orioles, when Vida Blue pitched his first game at Yankee Stadium in '71, for Chambliss and Reggie, for Boone and Cone and Wells, for Tino and Brosius, when Leyritz homered in the ALDS against Seattle in the drizzle at one in the morning and everyone sang "New York, New York" and no one wanted to go home.

I asked my wife to marry me while standing on home plate. I wrote my mother's eulogy on a typewriter in the offices of *Yankees Magazine* for a memorial Mass that night in the church at Fordham University.

Before a little weekly Sunday morning radio show on WFAN intervened in 2003, I would attend Mass in the auxiliary locker room where Bob Sheppard himself would serve as lector. I convinced myself people attended that service as much to hear Bob speak in person as they did to satisfy their weekly obligation. After the Mass would end, I would walk out to the outfield, leave the Stadium, buy my Sunday papers on River Avenue and return, sitting in the bleachers behind Monument Park hours before game time in the stillness, gazing at the magnificence of this world-famous structure.

All the moments, large and small, I have spent in Yankee Stadium, culminated in my receiving the singular honor of joining one of the smallest clubs in this country: public address announcer, this past August, for a weekend of games against the Los Angeles Angels.

Sitting in Bob Sheppard's chair was akin to cleaning the table after the Last Supper.

That's my life in that building, never to be the same.

WILL WEISS

Bob Sheppard's voice, since 1951, when he became the public address announcer at the old Yankee Stadium, was as integral to the fabric of the building as the short porch in right field, the black bleachers, and the pinstripes on the home team's white uniforms.

Sheppard was universally respected. Everyone except, to my knowledge, the late Eddie Layton, called him "Mr. Sheppard." I said hello to Mr. Sheppard on my first Yankee Stadium assignment as editor of YESNetwork.com, and he said hello back. He said hello to everyone. That always stuck with me.

I observed Mr. Sheppard routinely leave his post during the seventh-inning stretch because his introduction to "God Bless America" was pre-recorded; his sprint to the elevator in the loge section right after the game was as amazing—you'd never believe the speed of a nonagenarian—as it was humorous. Once the elevator reached the lobby he would disappear out the door past security and into Lot 14.

My most enduring memory of the Stadium, and of Mr. Sheppard, came in 2002: a chance encounter in the press dining room where I ended up sitting at a table with Mr. Sheppard and Hall of Fame broadcaster Ernie Harwell before a night game against the Tigers. After I finished gathering my pre-game information in the clubhouse, I headed in for some dinner before going up to the YES Network booth to write my early notebook. I couldn't find an empty table, and, still being a newcomer among the regular and semi-regular writers on site, I hadn't befriended too many local writers yet. The only available seat was at a table with Sheppard and Harwell. I approached the table and asked, "Is this seat taken?"

"No, young fella," Harwell said in his familiar, folksy tone.

I sat down with my tray, trembling. I'm not one to get star-struck, but this was Harwell and Sheppard—legends in sports and sports broadcasting. For me, an aspiring sportscaster at the time, this was a surreal scene. My junior year of college, when I moonlighted as the public address announcer for the UCLA baseball team, I had Sheppard on the brain every at bat of every game. A year later, when I was back at school and broadcasting baseball games for the college radio station, I tried to emulate Harwell's style.

Harwell, with his horn-rimmed coke-bottle frames, sat to my left while Sheppard, long face and a professorial demeanor, was on my right. I did not feel worthy of being in their presence and I tried like hell to control my emotions and hide my self-deprecation. I wanted to ask them both about 1951: Harwell's work with the Giants—specifically his TV call of the "Shot Heard 'Round the World" on NBC—and Sheppard on his first year as the Yankees' PA announcer, introducing Mantle and DiMaggio. There wasn't enough time.

Sadly, one thing I don't remember from the dinner was the topic of conversation. I didn't speak much, but I also know I didn't talk while chewing, so at least my manners were intact. I listened and tried to process it all. Maybe one of them would say something profound and I could learn something in a hurry. But the only thing that hurried was the clock. Five, maybe six minutes went by before Harwell announced his departure for the booth. Those five or six minutes felt like thirty seconds. He shook my hand, smiled, and wished me luck in my career. Harwell and Sheppard then exchanged adieus and a joke that could be understood only through fifty-plus years of friendship. Sheppard left about a minute later to continue his pregame routine and told me to have a good game. I wished him the same.

Over the next four-and-a-half seasons I had the privilege to cover many more regular season and playoff games, but there would not be another chance to share a meal—or part of one—with Bob Sheppard and Ernie Harwell. It's probably better that way. Moments like that should only happen once in a lifetime.

ED ALSTROM

My lasting memory of Yankee Stadium is getting to hang out with Bob Sheppard.

Mr. Sheppard—that's what all of us in the press box call him—has his public address booth right next to mine at the organ. Only a pane of Plexiglas separates us. Sometimes I'll knock on his door, sometimes he'll tap on my window and motion me in, and we chat, sometimes during the game. He'll be talking, and then point his index finger in the air mid-sentence, to say "wait a minute," step on a pedal to activate the mike, announce the next player (in the same exact tone of voice he's speaking to me in), and then continue where he left off. When a Yankee makes an error or a bad play, he'll look at me and very slowly point his palms skyward and shrug his shoulders.

His end of game routine is really beautiful: with two out in the ninth and Mariano on the hill, he'll slowly don his cap and coat, salute me, lock his door, and wait in the runway. If the game ends then and there, he is off like a shot, walking so briskly I can barely keep up with him—and I've tried it! If that batter reaches base, though, he'll unlock the door, come back in, give me that same shrug, step on the pedal, announce the next batter, and repeat the procedure. His determination to beat that traffic (and his success rate, I'm sure) is admirable indeed.

Several times, I've gone down to the press lunch room and broken bread with him at "his table," which is the one in the corner of the room with a cardboard handwritten sign with his name on it. He surely deserves a gold plaque or something more dignified (well, he does have a Monument in the Park).

You've probably heard what a class act he is, and he exceeds all expectations on that count. I've spoken to him many times, but it's almost never about baseball; usually music and theater. In fact, he usually changes the subject to music when I try to engage him about baseball.

He loves the music of the forties and the big bands. He told me once he was especially fond of the great singer Jo Stafford, so I went home and found a bunch of her recordings and put them on CD for him, and he was delighted and talked about her at length, about how he was stationed in Aruba during World War II, and they used to get her 78s shipped to them, and play them at their bar in the "Quonset hut" (you can just hear Shep saying "Quonset hut," right?).

He loves poetry, and is enamored of the lyrics of Hart, Hammerstein, Gershwin, Porter, et al. I've spent some time at his behest trying to explain the merits of rock and roll, or any music recorded after 1955, with limited success.

At times, he'll approach me with some handwritten poetry he's composed, which is invariably literate, funny, and sometimes biting. He once wrote a concise and venomous little masterpiece about Kevin Brown's bout with a cinder-block wall, and showed it to me; I am not at liberty to disclose it, but lemme tell you, it's incredible. I said to him, "You must have a lot of these." He said, "Oh, hundreds." I said, "You should get these published," to which he replied, "Oh, no, Mr. Stein-brenner would fire me!"

One Saturday afternoon, it was Military Day at the Stadium, and the formalities were to begin with the Golden Knights parachuting onto the field. It was about two minutes before the ceremony was to begin, and Mr. Sheppard was nowhere in sight.

I knocked on the control room window, got the director's attention, and pointed to myself and then to Shep's booth. He said, "Yeah, go ahead." So, I gave the script a speed read, got the cue, stepped on the pedal to activate the mike, and very deliberately said ". . . *Good afternoon, ladies and gentlemen; welcome to Yankee Stadium!*"

Now, I didn't have time to think about it, but my instinct was to not attempt my Shep imitation, because I felt it would be disrespectful, but I did try to phrase it as he might have, veer a course somewhere down the middle vocally, and create the illusion that it was him.

It was a very long script, about two pages, a real roller coaster moment. Toward the end of it, I noticed out of the corner of my eye that Mr. Sheppard was standing behind me! I finished, released the pedal, and looked at him gingerly, feeling like a child about to be scolded. Instead, he grinned and said very slowly, "Were you trying to imitate me?" Imagine that thrill!

But the best of all was when he approached me one day, and said, "You know, I wrote a song many years ago." Of course, I wanted to hear it, so he showed me the lyrics and sang it to me. I told him the next day I was coming back with a recorder, and he sang it again for me, a capella, and then I got him to talk into the recorder for about fifteen minutes about it. I then went home and created a musical track for his melody, chopped his vocal track into pieces and flew it in over the accompaniment, and presented him with a finished product worthy of Sinatra. He was moved, and I was touched to be able to do that for him. He wrote a handwritten note of thanks, which is more valuable to me than any piece of memorabilia. Believe me, Mr. Sheppard, the pleasure was all mine.

Whatever our collective vignettes are of Yankee Stadium, Bob Sheppard's narration to that soundtrack is a thread that runs through all of them. His humanity, wit, and warmth are every bit as momentous as that voice, and I am honored to have shared some time on this Earth with him. He *is* Yankee Stadium.

DAVE KAPLAN

My warmest memory of Yankee Stadium is of a rainy and chilly Opening Day in April of 1999, the day Yogi Berra finally came home.

It was a day many waited for and feared might never happen. For fourteen years, Yogi, a man always at peace with himself, never buckled under constant pressure to return to the place where he'd become such a beloved legend. I learned a lot about Yogi in my job as director of the Yogi Berra Museum & Learning Center. Mostly I learned that beyond his warm and fuzzy public image, he's about integrity and respect, a man of honor.

And being dishonored by George Steinbrenner two weeks into the 1985 season, when he was fired as manager without the courtesy of a face-to-face meeting or personal phone call, rubbed him badly. Yogi's subsequent self-imposed exile—he quietly vowed never to return as long as the Boss was in charge—was admired by legions. He was the Yankee who couldn't be bought.

Fast-forward fourteen years when George flew up from Tampa in the dead of winter to our Museum in New Jersey. He came seeking forgiveness, in person, for one of "the worst mistakes I ever made." Yogi graciously accepted his apology in a private meeting, and slyly hinted he would return to Yankee Stadium.

So he did. Yogi and his wife Carmen were encircled by TV crews and photographers outside the Stadium. I was nervous and excited for him as he was ushered into the employee entrance. He was wearing an overcoat and blue blazer and a baseball tie, and ambled his way down the steps into the Stadium's underbelly, through the twisting corridors to the Yankee clubhouse. I walked alongside him and he almost seemed a little lost, not familiar with the surroundings. Later he admitted to a case of Opening Day nerves.

Yogi made his rounds in the clubhouse, warmly greeted by players who'd never met him. Old friends like Joe Torre, Don Zimmer, and Mel Stottlemyre embraced this gnome of a man whose remarkable life and history were so intertwined with Yankee Stadium.

Finally, as the Yankees gathered in the dugout for the pre-game ceremonies, which included the raising of the 1998 championship banner, there Yogi sat on the bench. Players walked by patting him on the leg for good luck. Then Bob Sheppard, in his inimitable style, created a hush in the crowd when he said, "Now let's welcome back a special guest . . ."

He listed Yogi's extraordinary accomplishments, including his record ten world championships, and called him "a source of inspiration to his teammates . . . a man of conviction . . . Let's welcome back," said Sheppard, his voice rising, "Yogi Berra, Number 8." The Stadium erupted. I was allowed to watch from the corner of the dugout as Yogi walked to the mound in a driving rain where David Cone applauded into his glove. He shook Cone's hand and tossed the first pitch to Joe Girardi, who rushed toward him with the ball. "Thanks Yogi, this is a real thrill," he said. Then as Yogi walked off, he gave a half-wave to the crowd which was still standing and chanting, "Yogi . . . Yogi . . . Yogi." For the man famous for saying it ain't over till it's over, it was finally over. Yogi Berra was back in Yankee Stadium.

ALAN SCHWARZ

I creaked open the metal door to the visitors' clubhouse as if I had happened upon Al Capone's hideout. I was in the bowels of Yankee Stadium, age twenty-three and on my first assignment to cover a Major League Baseball game. I had every reason to think that multimillionaire ballplayers greeted rookie writers as warmly as they did hanging curveballs.

As I crept into the Blue Jays' locker room, I looked upon the two dozen men in various states of undress and felt like Admiral Stockdale. (Who am I? Why am I here?) But I mustered up the gumption to approach Joe Carter, the Toronto slugger who was busily putting on his uniform. He was an enormous man, with a side-of-beef neck, who surely could have taken me between his thumb and forefinger and squished me into oblivion. I held my notebook down near my waist and moved forward slowly. But he spotted me, and struck. "Hi, I'm Joe Carter," he smiled, turning to offer his hand. "How ya doin'?"

After picking up my notepad, which was sitting on the carpet next to my jaw, I proceeded to have one of the more pleasant conversations—about baseball or anything else—of my life. With a random ballplayer. And to be honest, they've never really stopped. I have the same memories as so many other folks of Yankee Stadium. My first game, on September

29, 1979, when for Fan Appreciation Day the team gave away random, leftover promotional items. (I spelled it "Willie Randolf" in my scorebook.) Cherishing Phil Linz's autograph, even though I had no idea who he was. Just imagining all the great players who had been on that field: Ruth, DiMaggio, Williams, Greenberg, Koufax. So what if I was subjected to Mel Hall and Oscar Azocar? It was Yankee Stadium. (Believe it or not, as I write this, I am in the press box watching the opening ceremonies before the first game at the new Yankee Stadium across the street. Dozens of retired Yankees are being introduced, and Horace Clarke received a bigger ovation than Reggie Jackson. I think that proves my point. Clarke is all but a symbol of the dreadful late-1960s Yankees, but so what? To people who grew up then, he'll always symbolize the summer they fell in love with baseball.)

The thing is, my memories of Yankee Stadium will never be the same as the fan I once was. I walked the hallways that the players did, stood inside the dugout, talked at the players' lockers. Pedro Martinez, recalling his days learning English on the buses of the Pioneer League. Nomar Garciaparra, remembering how he cherished the first real glove his dad bought him. Talking strategy with Greg Maddux, literature with Scott Rolen. I could go on and on. Whatever the often sanctimonious press would have you believe, I have found players to be wonderfully thoughtful and engaging. I'm convinced that there's the same percentage of jerk ballplayers as there are jerk stockbrokers, jerk plumbers and, well, jerk sportswriters. At this point you're surely thinking that the players grant me long interviews because they need me, a fallacy borne of a long-ago time when it was somewhat true—before television and guaranteed salaries. Players don't need writers anymore. They deal with us because it's part of the job, and because they're usually decent folks who respect someone trying to do his job as well as they do theirs.

I learned this by working in almost every baseball stadium in the country, and about a dozen that are long gone. But Yankee Stadium drove it home more than anywhere else. Will I miss the place I attended my first major league game? Not really. But when the old place comes down and I drive past what's left on the Major Deegan, I'll always see a spot where the visitors' clubhouse once stood, site of my first major league interview. It's so, Joe.

KEN ROSENTHAL

My favorite memory is the Jeffrey Maier game in the 1996 ALCS. I was a columnist for the *Baltimore Sun* at the time, but I grew up in New York. My father originally is from the Bronx, and when we would play one-on-one basketball or compete in something else, he would always invoke "Bronx Rules." Which is to say, no rules! So, after that game, I explained to the good people of Baltimore the concept of "Bronx Rules." And I wrote that the only way to fight them would be for the Orioles' crowd to play by "Bronx Rules" when the ALCS returned to Baltimore. In short, I was trying to incite a riot, basically. But of course, nothing changed.

After coming home to Baltimore, I remember sitting at breakfast with my son Sammy, who was five years old at that time. I asked him if he had heard about what happened to the Orioles in New York, about the kid who interfered with the ball. He looked at me and said, "I hate that kid." And I thought, "Awright!"

JOHNETTE HOWARD

I have indelible memories of plenty of nights at Yankee Stadium, especially the 2001 World Series—easily the most amazing set of baseball games I ever covered. But the unromantic truth is, to me, over the first ten years I worked in New York, the Stadium always felt like the House That George Built, not Ruth or Mantle or Jeter. George Steinbrenner built the Yankees into an unapolgetic business behemoth by the time I arrived at the tail end of their most recent dynasty. While Jeter usually needed a good game to change the mood at the Stadium, Steinbrenner often just needed to show up. Suddenly every security guard and elevator operator, every beat writer and Yankee staffer was on high alert. You could feel the frission of tension.

The night of June 13, 2000, was typically amusing. A version of this story about the Boss first appeared in a column I wrote for Newsday.

* * *

You knew he'd resurface soon, doing that Master-of-the-Universe walk of his with his chest stuck out like the prow of a battleship as he cleaves his way through the stadium corridor. Doesn't George Steinbrenner always show at a time like this?

The Boss was at the ballpark last night for the belated start of this week's much-anticipated Yankees–Red Sox series and—nothing personal—it was sad to see.

When the Yankees were rained out the previous two nights, it started to become delicious fun to sit back and read the carefully worded, mostly unattributed tea-leaf readings about Steinbrenner's latest mood swings. It was presumed he couldn't wait to swoop in and make a big gesture to fix things. The Yankees' recent travails have been an in-house cause for concern. And the longer the Boss stayed away, saying nothing, not even showing his face, the more wonderfully exaggerated and bombastic a figure he became, the more inflated his rage and his desire to win and his famous appetite for success all grew.

No one really talked on the record. They didn't dare. George was just "said to be" furious. He was "said to be" wagging a finger and shrieking "I told you so!" at the confidants who talked him out of the Jim Edmonds trade.

The longer the rainy days here dragged on, and the longer nothing changed since last weekend's series split with the Mets, the easier it was to imagine Steinbrenner sitting up in bed in his undershirt in the middle of the night, then causing the telephones to jingle off the nightstands of his three de facto general managers, Brian Cashman, Gene Michael, and Mark Newman, because he had three AM marching orders for them: "Dammit Stick, get me the scouting info on the Cubs! . . . Newman, get me the lowdown on Juan Gonzalez. . . . And Cashman, for God sakes, don't just sit there! What do we need? Pitching or hitting? Hitting or pitching?"

"What will it be?" Steinbrenner asked Yankees manager Joe Torre when they huddled in Torre's office before the game.

Right about here you may be wondering why one team, even the two-time defending world champion Yankees, need three ersatz GMs to jump when Steinbrenner roars? But isn't it obvious? They're human sandbags, a firewall against disaster at times like this, when George is "said to be" contemplating whether to trade half the roster and/or half the farm system (again) for—what'll it be?—suddenly available Cubs slugger Sammy Sosa or the Tigers' rent-a-star, Gonzalez? Gonzalez or Brad Radke? Or, since we're at this, why not Sosa and Gonzalez and Radke and—"CASHMAN! For God's sake, get me the scouting report on Schilling. What'll it take to dynamite him out of Philly?"

A sterling outing against Boston by Yankees starter Orlando Hernandez could've tempered the hand-wringing about where the Yankees are headed. But El Duque was only average last night. The Red Sox pecked him to death with a bloop here, a parachute double there. Then catcher Jason Varitek, the eighth hitter in the Red Sox order, provided the death blow in the sixth, working his way back from a 1-and-2 count to send a two-run homer climbing off toward the rightfield upper deck to give the Red Sox a 5-3 lead that Boston made stand up.

It has hardly matters that the Yankees came into the game in first place, or that it's only mid-June.

There is clamoring for the Yankees to add another power hitter though they've done just fine without a slugger like Sammy Sosa in the past. But the Mets and Red Sox are also interested in Sosa. And you know what the Boss says when the only thing standing between him and a big name who fascinates him is a little word like Y–E–S.

If you guessed something like—"Cashman, Get me Sosa, dammit! And if I'm wrong, you're fired!"—you win!

When Steinbrenner brushed by in the hallway I asked, "George, what'll it be?"

"Well we better do SOMETHING," Steinbrenner barked. "Don't you think?"

BOB KLAPISCH

Everyone's got a farewell memory of Yankee Stadium, maybe a personal shrine. I'm no different: as I left the great ballpark for the last time on September 21, I said good-bye to an abstract soft spot in my heart that won't make it across the street.

I consider it a shrine without shape or form; it's just a place. Actually, it's just air-space, the spot right outside the Yankee clubhouse where David Wells was waiting to launch the most bizarre showdown of my career.

I've had my share of shoot-outs (See: Bobby Bonilla, 1993), but none that could've been reviewed by a journalism ethics class. Ok, a little background. In the summer of 1997, when I was still a beat reporter for the *Bergen Record* and one of the few writers who actually liked Boomer—I always considered him slightly larger than life, if not larger than his uniform—I caught wind of a explosive confrontation between the lefthander and George Steinbrenner.

It occurred in the ninth inning of a game the Yankees were losing to the lowly Expos, during which Wells had been knocked out. Steinbrenner, embarrassed that the defending world champs were getting punished by one of the National

League's worst teams, was pacing the clubhouse. He was in a terrible mood.

Wells wasn't happy, either. He started a conversation with the Boss that would soon make headlines.

"Hey, George, you need to get some security out there in right field. Build a wall or something," Wells said.

He was referring to a fan who'd leaned over the railing and prevented Paul O'Neill from catching Darrin Fletcher's second inning fly ball. The fan caught the ball and it was ruled a home run.

That was all the Boss needed to hear. The engine of his rage was now fully ignited:

> **Steinbrenner:** Never mind about the fucking security, you just worry about your pitching. You better start winning some games, because you're not the pitcher I thought you were.
> **Wells:** Is that right? Well, you can go fuck yourself. If you don't like it, you can trade me.
> **Steinbrenner:** Believe me, I would, but no one wants your fat ass.
> **Wells:** You better get the fuck out of this room, before I fucking knock you out.
> **Steinbrenner:** Go ahead, do it. Try it. You think I'm afraid of you?

Wells and Steinbrenner apparently eyeballed each other for another moment, before the tension defused. No punches were thrown.

How did I know all this? Three teammates and one of the Yankee trainers were in the clubhouse during the exchange—

two of whom couldn't wait to give me the blow-by-blow as soon as the game was over.

Wells was already gone, so I couldn't verify the quotes. But, given how much I trusted the two sources, I ran with the story—verbatim—in the next day's *Record*. It was a clean scoop, the kind a beat reporter dreams about. All the other papers, including the tabloids, were forced to follow it, which couldn't have made my editors any happier.

Boomer, however, was furious. He was waiting for me the next day at his locker, where we usually made small talk before batting practice. But not this time.

"Who told you about me and George?" Wells asked coldly. It was more of a threat than a question: our war was just beginning.

"You know I can't tell you, David," I said. "If you told me something in confidence, I'd respect that. It's called protecting your sources."

"Fuck that. I have to know who's the rat in this clubhouse," he said.

"Sorry," I said, even though I wasn't.

"Listen, you think about it during the game," Wells said. "You come down here afterwards and tell me who I can and can't trust. If you don't, we're done."

"Boomer, we're done," I said. "I can tell you that right now."

"Just think about it," he said, walking away.

There was no debate: a source is a source. I'm not sure I would've gone to jail to protect them, but luckily for me, I wasn't facing a judge after the game, only Boomer, who was too impatient to wait at his locker. There he was, at the door outside the room, like some hired muscle working the rope at a nightclub.

"What's it going to be, Bob?" he asked, closing in on my airspace.

"We're done, Boomer," I said, holding my ground.

"Fucking right we're done," Wells said, walking away. It was the last time we spoke, but that's not to say the big lefty was finished with this story. In fact, he himself became the leak, repeating the incident to anyone and everyone—his teammates as well as the rest of the League.

I watched with amusement about two weeks later, as Wells was standing with several Orioles during batting practice. He was roaring with laughter as he mimicked Steinbrenner's most cutting remark—"no one wants your fat ass."

Not true, of course. Wells' career lasted another 10 years, but true to his word, he never spoke to me again. He had his principles, I suppose, I had mine. Someday in his retirement Wells might realize I was right. But I'm not holding my breath.

ANTHONY McCARRON

It's strange, but most everything else about that night is a blur, dissolved into a torrent of deadline writing, scrambling around the clubhouse for quotes and later, in the Stadium press box, for the words to detail the looming Subway Series—this time, for real—that was coming between the Yankees and Mets.

All that furious effort, I don't remember any of it, not even hitting the computer button that would send my final story to the editors and signal the end of my workday. That the Yankees rallied from a 4–0 deficit, that the Mariners scored three times in the eighth to make it close again, and October pariah Alex Rodriguez was incredible for Seattle with four hits, including a homer and two doubles? Forgotten until recently when I looked at the box score.

But what I'll never forget is what happened after David Justice's Game 6 home run in the seventh inning of the 2000 ALCS against Seattle, the shot that essentially put the Yankees in the World Series yet again.

My God, the press box of the old place was shaking. Swaying. There were 56,598 souls in the stands that night, October 17, 2000, and all of them must have been stomping as

Justice rounded the bases, as they begged him to come out of
the dugout for a curtain call.

Frankly, it was unsettling and for more than just a single
moment. I stopped reworking my running game story—the
one that has to be to editors as quickly as possible once the
outcome is decided—and put my hand next to the computer
sitting in front of me to feel the vibrations. Yikes.

I was in my first season on the beat. I had worked the 1999
World Series and knew that the Stadium could get raucous, but
this was something else, scary and amazing at the same time.

Afterward, Justice, an affable fellow who mostly enjoyed
dealing with the press, talked about the indescribable—what
it's like to hit a huge home run in an important spot with the
baseball world watching. "I wish y'all could feel it," he said.

We can't, of course. For a moment, I had my own feeling in
its wake, though, just as memorable for me.

I have been at most of the epic events at the Stadium of the
last ten years or so, from dirty chapters of the Yankee–Red Sox
saga to late-night, story-busting home runs in the 2001 World
Series. But no memory has endured the same way. It is still the
first thing I think of when people ask about working so often
at Yankee Stadium.

DAVE KINDRED

This was October 2001 in New York.

I walked from the firehouse at Canal and Allen streets to the intersection of Broadway and Fulton. From there I could see the disfigured ribs of the steel skeleton once hidden by the tower's beauty.

Leaving, taking the subway north, past midtown, into the Bronx, I went to 161st Street.

There, Yankee Stadium.

I first stood in Yankee Stadium twenty-five years earlier. Your first time, you stand there. You look. Babe Ruth walked here, Gehrig, Mantle, all those guys on the monuments in center field. In some weird, beautiful pre-memory deal, you remember being in a place where you've never been. I was in Yankee Stadium on October 8, 1956, and I was a thousand miles away in a little town in Illinois where I skipped school, sat on the couch, kept score, and moved only when Dale Mitchell couldn't pull the trigger. With every pitch Don Larsen threw, I was in Yankee Stadium.

Now, October 2001, Yankee Stadium, and I was a reporter with a notebook asking Tino Martinez what it was like to be a Yankee. His time in New York was near an end; he was thirty-three years old, expendable. He had been a big Yankee, six years, 175 home runs.

"Whatever happens, happens," he said. Then he answered me: "The Yankees are what baseball is all about."

That night, he went to bat, two runs down, his team about to lose a third game in the World Series, and he went up intending to hit it out. He said, "I looked for something I could turn on and take a good, strong hack at it."

First pitch, gone.

I'll remember that moment at Yankee Stadium, an earthquake of joy. Soon enough, another home run, and the Yankees won. And the next night, again, a ninth inning home run to tie a game they would win. And a Rabbi Ephraim Z. Buchwald wrote to the *New York Times*: "The events of recent days raise some ponderous theological questions. With so much going on in the world, why is God spending so much time with the New York Yankees?"

This was October 2001 in Yankee Stadium.

Firefighters and police officers stood on that field in dress uniform.

The assembled tens of thousands sang "God Bless America" as preamble to "Take Me Out to the Ball Game."

And that night, like little boys wishing to be their heroes, the Yankees took the field wearing caps that bore the legends "FDNY" and "NYPD."

The morning after the Tino Martinez game, the hotel maid who had come from Puerto Rico to make a life in New York said her son was seven years old and loved baseball and went to bed the night before without knowing what happened. So she told him, "The Yankees win," and he was happy, and as she told the story, she asked me, "Who do you want to win?"

I pointed to a Yankees cap on a chair by the desk. In October 2001, Yankee Stadium was more than a ballpark. Maybe, for once, it was the cathedral we sportswriters always claimed it to be. I bought the cap because it represented more than a city's team, it represented an idea. You get knocked down, you get up.

"Of course, you are a Yankees fan," she said.

And I asked her to take my cap home to her son.

MIKE VACCARO

What I'll always remember most are the eyes: eyes belonging to professional baseball players, who aren't supposed to be impressed by much and are surprised by even less. Eyes filling a clubhouse containing men who had already won three consecutive World Series and eleven consecutive playoff series and were already being listed among the greatest dynasties of all time.

And yet late on the night of November 1, 2001, and early in the morning of November 2, those eyes were all rheumy and moist and wide with wonder. Even the Yankees couldn't believe what they'd just seen, and done. Even the Yankees couldn't quite fathom that, a night after Tino Martinez had rescued them with a two-out, two-run home run in the bottom of the ninth inning in Game 4, Scott Brosius had done the same exact thing, taken Byung-Hyun Kim deep and sent Yankee Stadium into the kind of frenzy that you can still summon in your ears, and your memory, all these years later.

I remember it especially well because it is the only time in twenty years as a newspaperman that I've ever blown an edition. I was working for the *Newark Star-Ledger* at the time, and had written a "running" column which described how valiantly the Yankees had fought in losing and going down three games to two in the Series, and I'd done so without composing a backup "early" column in case it didn't work out that way.

But it was clear: lightning had struck once the night before.

Couldn't happen again.

And then it did.

I had already left the press box to stand outside the Yankees clubhouse, to avoid the rush and the crush of postgame. There was a TV monitor set up there, which was on a four-or-five second delay. Which helped add to the surreal nature of the moment, because Kim was still in the stretch position on TV when suddenly there emerged from the tunnel leading to the home dugout a roar that defied explanation. And could mean only one thing.

"No fucking way," said one of my colleagues.

"You've got to be fucking shitting me!" said another.

And then we saw on TV what the 55,000 on the other side of the dugout had just seen: Brosius laying into one, releasing the bat, raising his arms, unleashing the kind of primal joy that defies description. It had only been a few days earlier when Derek Jeter, talking about one of his favorite subjects, had said, "Just wait until the ghosts start acting up around here."

And then they had.

And you know what's funny? It really doesn't matter that the ghosts didn't make the trip back to Arizona with them two days later, that Game 5 would be the last game the Yankees would win in 2001, that they would lose Game 7 in a manner every bit as excruciating. Because for so many, Game 5 would stand alone as a moment in time when baseball—and, appropriately, Yankee Stadium—would be a part of something greater than themselves.

Obviously, there was the still-smoldering wreckage at Ground Zero adding poignancy to the picture. There were millions of grieving New Yorkers, and tens of millions of hurting Americans, who turned to baseball in that time, a way to spend three hours away from the brutality of reality. All of that probably explains the foundation-shaking din that emerged from the throats of those 55,000 fans.

And, of course, it was also just one hell of a baseball moment.

My favorite of all time, regardless of where it had happened. It just happened to happen in the only place it should have happened.

PETE CALDERA

We've talked and talked, and asked and asked about Yankee Stadium memories for months. What will you recall most? What will you take? And then Derek Jeter reminded us of an underrated—and unforgettable—treasure.

It's the view.

From the batter's box, for a thousand games, Jeter tapped home plate and stared straight toward the black batter's eye—a perfect hitter's backdrop. And from the front row of the press box, I was lucky to take in the whole panorama from behind home plate.

You couldn't always see what was going on in the corners, but any member of the BBWAA was granted one of the best seats in the old house. The dugouts, the mound, the infield, the on-deck circle were all right in front of you. The battles in the stands—for foul balls, or for disputes—were in clear view. Occasionally, some daredevil drunk would even drop out of his box seat and land on the netting in front of us (happened twice).

The Bronx County Courthouse on a clear day. The moon rising from left field on a clear night. It was all right there. And then, of course, there was that grand, green field—and I'll count myself forever fortunate to have witnessed some precious moments on that celebrated turf.

I was there for David Wells's perfect game, on a cloudy May afternoon. Remember that backhand stab by Chuck Knoblauch, of all people?

Saw an unassisted triple play by Randy Velarde.

Saw David Cone's perfect game, and remember telling a friend during a rain delay (thirty-three minutes) that it was too bad—Cone's slider was unhittable. He could no-hit the Expos.

Saw Mussina save the day in Game 7, the night Pedro was left to battle through the eighth inning, and couldn't. Then, Aaron Boone. And bedlam.

Saw Pedro come within a Chili Davis homer of perfection, still the greatest-pitched game I ever witnessed.

Saw the Red Sox win the pennant. Saw plenty of brawls—like the night Strawberry seemed to take on the entire Orioles team in the visiting dugout. Saw Jeter in the hole, whirling and throwing. And saw hundreds of his two-thousand-plus hits. And saw him go for that pop-up, in fair territory, against Boston, knowing that his only landing area was full-speed into the stands.

Saw A-Rod make the Stadium small with those colossal home runs, and wished I could've seen Joe D. swing for the deeper fences—the original dimensions.

Saw the first Subway Series game, and the first Mets-Yankees World Series game.

Saw Joe Torre do that slow walk to the mound. Saw DiMaggio wave from a convertible. Saw the Florida Marlins celebrate, and heard them too, in the silence. Saw the All-Star Game that never ended.

I witnessed all that from the press box, mostly from Seat 12, behind a red plate with "The Record" in white lettering.

The Yankees are giving the writers those plates. And from where that plate once stood, I'll never forget the view.

JOE POSNANSKI

OK, look, I don't really have a lasting Yankee Stadium memory. I mean, sure, I have them, but they're no different than the 5,483,794 lasting Yankee Stadium memories that have been told the last six months or six years or six decades or however long this "Lasting Yankee Stadium Memory" series has been running.

So the only reason I'm even writing this is because Alex pretty much bullied me into it by noodging me about it three times a day, every day since before my second child was born. I just assumed he would forget about it at some point, assumed that even for him the expiration date on Yankee Stadium memories would pass, assumed that he would let me live in peace. No. This man, like Billy Martin, simply knows no peace. I am of the firm belief now that that the best way to find Osama Bin Laden is to have Alex Belth assign him a "Lasting Yankee Stadium Memory" essay.

Anyway, what kind of unique Yankee Stadium memory does Alex even think I have? Who am I, Robert Merrill? Hey, maybe my memory was the time that me and the other short-pants kids in the Bronx skipped school and slipped past the front guards at the stadium and caught the last of Larrupin' Lou's three homers, which just so happened to heal my sick little brother Tommy. Or maybe it was that day in '78 when I was a kid sitting outside the Stadium and Billy Martin first threatened to hit me in my fat face and then apologized (said he had confused me for "Steinbrenner or one of them") and then invited me to sit by him and tell Reggie he was benched.

Or maybe, seven years old, and my dad takes me to Yankee Stadium. My first game. We go in through this long, dark tunnel underneath the stands. And I'm holding his hand, and we come out of the tunnel, into the light. It was huge. How green the grass was, the brown dirt, and that great green copper roof, remember? We had a black-and-white TV then, so this was the first I ever saw in color. I sat there the whole game next to my dad. He taught me how to keep score. Mickey hit one out.

Yeah. Memories. Not my memories. But at this point does it even matter? Others have told all of my memories. Sure, I was there the night when Jeter hit the November homer and listened to the recording of Frank singing "These little town blues . . ." again and again and again. I was there when John Wetteland went to the mound—this had to be three or four hours after he had gotten Mark Lemke to pop out to clinch the Yankees first World Series in a generation. The Stadium was almost empty, and Wetteland stepped on the mound, and he just looked around . . . it was like he wanted just one more look.

I was there to hear Bob Sheppard say "Yankee Way," I was there to see DiMaggio's two-hand wave, I was there to hear a real Bronx Cheer—and it is true that all others taste like grape juice to that fine wine. I was there to see Greg Maddux at his baffling best, there to see perhaps the second-greatest team in baseball history destroy the Padres, there to see David Cone throw one of the guttsiest games I've ever watched, there to see Albert Belle snap at some fans, there to catch a glimpse of

Bruce Springsteen, there to see George Steinbrenner, there to see Spike Lee, there to see Rudy Giuliani, there to see Mariano Rivera close the door.

And, yes the memory that Alex probably wanted, I stood in the rain in center-field back in 1996, the day that Game 1 of the World Series was rained out. I stood out there where (more or less) DiMaggio stood, the Mick, Bobby, Mick the Quick, Bernie, Jerry Mumphrey. I looked around, took it all in, listened for the echoes, looked for the ghosts, all of that. There were a few policemen standing in the rain too, and I thought they were going to come get me, but they seemed to understand what I was doing.

In fact, as I trudged in I passed one of them. He said: "Getting your Lasting Yankee Stadium Memory for Belth, right?" New York police officers are wise.

STEVE RUSHIN

B eing a sportswriter is like being a big-league baseball player, only without the money, fame, women, physical gifts, and steroids. But they're alike in one way: Five minutes after I entered Yankee Stadium for the very first time, I was standing in the Yankees clubhouse, sitting in the Yankees dugout, and walking onto the Yankee Stadium grass, wondering when security would arrest me for trespassing.

It was like stepping into the NBC *Game of the Week*, stepping into the twenty-four-inch Zenith TV set of my Minnesota family room circa 1978. The first time I walked from the visitors' dugout to the batting cage before a game at the Stadium I had to restrain myself from breaking into a sprint and attacking home plate umpire Tim McClelland, even though he wasn't there. It was impossible to cover that ground without thinking of George Brett, in 1983, giving new meaning to the phrase "going batshit."

Even so, the strongest memories I have of Yankee Stadium aren't the first ones. I'll never forget heading from the auxiliary press seats to the clubhouse level in the eighth inning of Game 6 of the 2003 World Series while trying to avoid the crush of the postgame crowd. Barring a late rally against Josh Beckett, the Yankees were about to lose the Series to the Marlins. I got on an empty elevator and descended a floor. The elevator doors opened and a man got on. It was Yogi Berra. And all I could think was: This one really is over before it's over.

I'll take a lot of memories from the Stadium. But the Stadium has also taken from me. And this what I'll remember most. I had just flown back from covering the 2000 Summer Olympics in Sydney when I more or less went straight to the Stadium on October 6 for Game 3 of the American League Division Series. I was a spectator for this one, a 4–2 win over the A's, and after the game I stepped jet-lagged out of the Stadium, heading for the D train, when I realized that I didn't have my cell phone. In the fog of the previous twenty-four hours of flying, I had lost it somewhere in the Stadium.

I called my number from a friend's phone. It rang and rang. I called it the next night, during the library-silence of the A's 11–1 rout of the Yankees. It continued to ring. I haven't a clue where in the Stadium my phone was ringing, but over the next few days I continued to call it. I don't know what I expected: Perhaps the voice of Bob Sheppard to pick up and say, "Yankee Stadium, how may I direct your call?" But it never happened and I finally had the phone declared legally dead and got a new one.

But ever since that October night, I like to think my old oversized Nokia remained hidden somewhere in the Stadium, an earwitness to history, lodged in some obscure corner untouched by cleaning crews. I like to think it's buried there at the Stadium site even now, a ghostly bullpen phone that will never be answered.

JEFF PEARLMAN

My family hated baseball.

That was the worst thing about growing up a sports fan at 24 Emerald Lane in Mahopac, New York. My mom could not care less about sports. My dad could not care less about sports. My brother could not care less about sports.

Me? I cared. Boy, did I care. My walls were lined with one poster after another—Rickey Henderson next to Wesley Walker next to George Foster next to Bernard King. My closets were stuffed—stuffed!—with baseball cards, thirty . . . forty together, rubber-banded in ways that left Mario Soto and Dan Pasqua positioned in the most awkward of poses. Dozens of baseball caps lined up neatly behind my bed.

But nobody cared.

Then, one day, my dad asked if I had any interest in going to a Yankees game. It was 1985 and Rich Green, one of his employees at Herz Stewart & Co., had an extra ticket. "You guys both love baseball," Dad said. "He wants to take you."

I still remember walking into the stadium that first time. We sat along the third-base line, and my posters had come to life. There was Ken Griffey Sr., his hat tipped high atop the front of his Afro, stretching calves the size of large dogs. There was Henderson, the great base stealer, twitching his fingers into white batting gloves. There was Henry Cotto, uhm, well, yeah. Henry Cotto. The grass was as green as a 7-Up label, Bob Sheppard's voice even more God-like then the one I'd heard on TV all those times. My seat was made of a hard blue plastic, and as the innings passed I must have bounced up and down upon it, oh, five hundred times. Like Victor Mata, I was just happy to be there.

I've been told a game was even played that day. I recall little of it, only that Dave Winfield made an amazing leaping catch into the right-field stands and that Butch Wynegar started at catcher. Doesn't matter, though. What sticks with me is the magic of the day; the feeling of walking into a building and knowing love.

True love.

DAVE ZIRIN

I t was ours.

    My father was smitten by the Dodgers of Brooklyn. He grew up near Ebbets Field and raised me with stories of the 1955 World Series champions the way other kids might hear about Robin Hood.

To my dad's telling, the Dodgers were more than a team, they were "a movement for the little guy." Jackie, Duke, and Pee Wee were leading the forces of righteousness against a Yankee team, the U.S. Steel of the sport.

That's what I learned at my father's knee so, of course, I was a Yankee fan. The Dodgers may had long gone to Chavez Ravine and those pinstripes were a perpetual irritation, but that just made the Yankees ever more essential. Much to his chagrin, I insisted on being at the Stadium.

I grew up watching the team in the 1980s, that painful decade where the Bombers led the major leagues in wins without taking a pennant after 1981. But they still had the swagger: Winfield, Mattingly, Guidry, Righetti. They were giants.

Entering Yankee Stadium meant primarily seeing my heroes. The Stadium was a backdrop, no more no less. I'd like to say it was like entering a cathedral or a magical monument to greatness but no. It just always "was."

Since Yankee Stadium was my first stadium, I had no perspective. Only after I first entered Shea did I realize what we had in the Bronx. I can't believe it seems to have left more with a whimper than with a bang. I am struck by the absence of sentiment. Ralph Nader, the Yankee fan from Connecticut said, "Would they bulldoze Carnegie Hall?" Imagine if the city political leaders and team owners of the Chicago Cubs and the Boston Red Sox tried to level Wrigley Field or Fenway Park. Fans in those cities would be chaining themselves to the wrecking balls. Armed with only a beer and a bratwurst they would be doing their best impression of Tiananmen Square. It would all make the 1968 Democratic convention look like a church picnic. And yet Yankee Stadium, the eighty-eight year-old "House That Ruth Built," the most championship-laden club in all of sports has now closed its doors with nary a whimper. From ex- and current players, to fans in the Bronx, to the tweedy, misty-eyed, baseball cognoscenti, the collective sentiment was summed up simply by Yankee captain Derek Jeter: "It's time."

I just can't agree. It may never have had the ivy of Wrigley or the green monster of Fenway. It had only history. It was the scenery of the finest team sport achievements of the century. It also was ours.

The new Yankee Stadium will be "ours" in the sense that a billion of our tax dollars went into it. But the old Statium had something else, something I certainly fear will be forgotten.

MAGGIE BARRA

I vividly remember the first time I went to Yankee Stadium and looked out on the field. I was six; I know that because I got to leave my first grade class early. My father was already there; my mother and I joined him.

I remember being perplexed by the slanted ramps that seemed to never merge and were separated by black vertical bars. I remember the dark blue paint next to white everywhere and knowing that they were the Yankees' colors. I followed about two feet behind my mother. The game had already started, and most of the people were in their seats. There was a small square doorway resembling a miniature tunnel; the walls were navy again with a hint of shine that felt sticky and reminded me of rubber, especially against the unremarkable concrete floor.

There was a slight upward climb past the door. My mother's high heels clacked as she hurried, then suddenly she stopped at the edge, seeming to stand in the open with no roof over her. I came up behind her and saw it for the first time. Before I noticed the actual stadium, a deafening roar arose from all around me and a lit up sign announced HOME RUN! I had heard of a home run before, but wasn't sure what it meant, but I knew from the crowd's reaction that it was good.

I stood there, a little breathless as I managed to take in this very large, wonderful place. I noticed the green grass with a crisscross pattern, the white letter-looking sign behind home plate, the endless supply of people surrounding the field except for the spaces with no seats, and at the back, a black area underneath the scoreboard. The net behind the plate expanded like a spider web.

We found my dad, who was seated with friends, and he pointed out the bullpen where the pitchers practice. Next to that he showed me Monument Park, where there was a plaque for every great player who ever played for the Yankees and had his number retired. I assumed that they were buried there. I don't remember if the Yankees won or lost that night, but that doesn't matter; it was a wonderful night that I will always remember.

A little over a decade later, I took my last trip to Yankee Stadium. As I exited the elevated subway with my parents at the 161st Street stop and the train pulled away, I saw both the skeleton of the new stadium and the full-bodied old Yankee Stadium, the one of my memories. I felt sad looking at the old Yankee Stadium, like it knew it was now outdated in the eyes of its owners and was politely waiting to make way for the emerging replacement across the street. My father could recall when his father brought him to witness the 1961 Yankees, and it occurred to me why we are all so attached to this place.

Yankee Stadium—I hate saying the "old" Yankee Stadium—is like visiting your grandparents' house, every trip special, and you always came back with great stuff you didn't need but loved. My mom would say I had enough Yankees stuff already—as if that were possible!

I can remember almost every place I've ever watched a game at the Stadium, the people we met sitting near us (especially the nuns who left in disgust during one very nasty loss!), and great plays someone made that the rest of the world has forgotten, like the game against Toronto in 2004 where Miguel Cairo knocked down a line drive hit between first and second, crawled on his hands and knees to pick it up, and then flipped it to first for the out.

It was good to know that as our baseball heroes grew older or were traded or simply faded, and as seasons passed without going to the World Series, the place where you witnessed all this history remained and would be there next year. It hurts to know that now there is no next year for my old friend, but life goes on. From my first visit at as a six-year-old in 1998 to my last visit at age seventeen in 2008, I will always remember the family friend of my grandfather, my father, and myself.

MARTY APPEL

As the days of Yankee Stadium wound down in September of 2008, there was a lot of talk about the majesty and perfection of the original, 1923-73 ballpark, and talk of how the remodeled park (1976-2008) paled in comparison.

I worked in both ballparks. Let me tell you, when the renovated one opened in 1976, nobody talked in disappointing terms. The feeling was that the new had captured the grandeur of the old, while adding the touches that made it more fan-friendly, not to mention safer. The old place, after all, was no longer structurally sound and needed repair.

What has been largely forgotten over time is the horrible obstructed view seats in the original park, with so many steel poles extending through each deck, causing horrible sight lines. In addition, there were no escalators, the rest rooms were antiquated, the place was developing a seedy quality, and it wasn't attractive to fans. Barely a million a year were trekking up to the Bronx.

It's like the nostalgia for Ebbets Field. Few remember how narrow and uncomfortable the seats were. Your knees bounced off your chest. It was a terrible place to see a game.

The new place opened to generally rave reviews, and two million came to see it in year one. It was the first time an American League team had drawn that many people in a quarter century. Baseball was beginning to find its sea legs in the mid '70s after a decade of lost ground to the NFL. An exciting '75 World Series set the table. A Yankee pennant in a new Yankee Stadium in 1976 really set baseball into its modern marketing era.

The introduction of luxury suites, a modern marvel scoreboard, and hey – unobstructed views from every seat – turned Yankee Stadium into a fan delight. On top of that, the team began to shine with star after star. They won ten pennants in the new Stadium, and although they won zero between 1982-1996, the team was always competitive, always had star power, and became worthy of Broadway show prices.

Munson and Jackson were followed by Winfield and Mattingly, and they were followed by Jeter and Williams and O'Neill and Rivera. With skilled role players, the roster was finely crafted to produce not only championships clubs – but also a likeable Yankee team – a new concept to a sports culture used to either loving or hating the Yankees.

To me, the only regret about the modernization was that it eliminated the ability to have Yankee Stadium declared a landmark, and to keep the concrete walls standing. I welcome the new stadium. No one ever expected the team to draw four million a year, and they just plain outgrew the current one.

But it would have been nice to see the concrete shell, the one that goes back to 1923, find a way of remaining, no matter what will ultimately come to be on the land itself.

BRUCE MARKUSEN

My father took me to my first game at Yankee Stadium in 1973. I was eight years old and it just so happened to be the final night game in the history of the original Yankee Stadium. More specifically, it was the night of September 28th, a Friday night, with the Yankees playing host to the venerable Detroit Tigers. Like the Yankees, the Tigers were playing out the string that fall, but they carried a royal bearing as the defending American League East Champions.

We had seats somewhere down the left-field line; I think they may have been in the reserved section. Man, I loved that Stadium, from its landmark façade, to the wonderful way the upper deck framed the ballpark, to the fading green color of the seats. It was both a stadium and a time machine. Though my father and I had an unobstructed view, some fans near us were positioned right behind one of the old Stadium's columns, which must have completely blocked their vantage point. (Some people call them posts or pillars, but we always referred to them as columns.) Those old columns, while they looked regal on TV or from a long distance, and gave the place the classic feel of a Roman coliseum, were just about the only drawback to the ballpark.

I'll always remember that game first and foremost for the fact that Woodie Fryman started for the Tigers. He was a pretty good left-hander, and gave up all four Yankee runs over six innings, despite having pitched a shutout through the first five frames. The Yankees' early offensive ineptitude against Fryman shouldn't have been surprising considering that Celerino Sanchez batted fifth in manager Ralph Houk's lineup. Yes, that Celerino Sanchez.

In the bottom of the sixth, with the Tigers leading 1–0, Fryman encountered his first stumbling block of the night, giving up a three-run homer to Bobby Murcer, who was one of my two favorite Yankees at the time, along with Thurman Munson. The Yankees then tacked on another run in the bottom of the seventh on an RBI single by, of all people, Horace "Hoss" Clarke. That would prove to be plenty of run support for Yankee ace Mel Stottlemyre, who pitched a complete-game pseudo-shutout, allowing only one unearned run against a Tigers lineup that featured old favorites like Norm Cash, Willie Horton, Gates Brown, and Bill Freehan. Hey, with players like "Stormin' Norman" and "Gator," it must have been fun to be a Tiger fan back then.

It was a comfortable late September night, and what I remember most is my father giving me lessons in baseball. He taught me a lot about the game, everything from how curve-balls used to be called "drops" to the importance of a field manager in establishing attitude and discipline on a team. That old-fashioned stadium, in the midst of a pleasant fall night, provided an ideal setting for a father and son to cross the generations, aided by the common theme of baseball.

Yes, that old Stadium served its purpose very well.

DIANE FIRSTMAN

My mom was born in the farm country of Monticello, New York, in the late 1920s. My dad was born in the Boro Park section of Brooklyn around the same time. They met when my mom moved to NYC after high school to find a job as a secretary. They married in 1958.

Some time shortly thereafter, my dad began exhibiting signs of mental illness, bouts of paranoia, and delusions. Amidst all this, I was born in 1963. It was obvious that my dad wasn't capable of being a caregiver to the family, so my mom got a quickie divorce in 1965, and my dad returned to live with his mother in Borough Park. My mom and I stayed in our apartment in Jackson Heights, Queens.

Dad had visitation rights, once a week at my apartment for a few hours on a Saturday or Sunday. He would hop on the B train, then the F, and upon arriving at our house, plop himself down on the couch and turn on the TV, invariably to the Yankee game on Channel 11 with Rizzuto, Messer, and White. My mom scolded him for this seeming lack of interaction with me. So, sometimes we'd ride the Q66 bus on Northern Boulevard out past Shea Stadium to Main Street in Flushing to do some shopping or see a movie in the (now boarded-up) RKO Keith theater.

I soon inferred that if I wanted to engage with dad, it was going to involve baseball, especially the Yankees. My dad heartily encouraged this. I took a fondness to Bobby Murcer, since he was the only "name" on those middling early seventies teams. So dad got me a T-shirt with an oversized Murcer head on a cartoon body. He knew I was good with numbers, so he got me a Strat-O-Matic game, and occasionally we sat down to play.

Our "big events" were schlepping on the train to Yankee Stadium (though, in my kid mind, we lived only fifteen minutes on the 7 train from Shea, why couldn't we go there?). In the early- to mid-seventies, before the Yanks made free agency their own version of *Candy Land*, you could easily walk up and grab a couple of field level seats on game day.

We went to Old Timers' Day often, and regardless of the particular day/game, we always sat on the third-base side, seemingly always behind one of the girders. I'd sit there with the program dad bought me, filling out the scorecard and attempting, in my own baseball shorthand, to keep score. Dad would enjoy a beer or two and a dog. We went to a couple of games at Shea while the Stadium was being renovated. I was there to see my guy Murcer finally connect for his first homer at Shea (one of only two he hit at Shea that year).

As I got a little bit older, I was able to go to games on my own. Of all the quirky events I've been witness to, seeing Bump Wills and Toby Harrah connect on back-to-back inside-the-park homers is pretty darn near the top of the list. One of my visits to the Stadium in 1978 saw Gator get his 20th victory (on his way to 25–3), a dominating five-hitter against the Tigers.

Dad became increasingly reclusive as he grew older, rarely venturing out of the house. He called little delis in the neighborhood to have groceries delivered and managed to find the one doctor in Borough Park that still made house calls. Our visits became more infrequent. I'd go out to his house and help clean his apartment. We'd watch whatever sporting event was on. He'd ask a few questions about how school was going, how my friends were doing, but I just didn't feel emotionally connected to him.

We did get to one final game at the "new" Stadium, Yankee Stadium II, together. Somehow, the tickets got lost in the mail, and the Yankee ticket office ended up giving us other seats in left field, just to the left of the foul pole, third row, on a blistering hot day. My dad made it through half of batting practice, and then told me that it was too hot, he was going home. I said I would go with him, but he insisted I stay, so I did.

Dad passed away in December 1994, amidst a garbage-strewn apartment in a building with neighbors who told me he stole their mail and threw pennies at their door. At his funeral, a cousin remarked that my dad should have been buried with a Yankee cap. "He loved those Yankees."

I've gone to a few games at the Stadium since then, mostly when someone comes up with free tickets or good seats. I was there for Opening Day in 2007. To my wonderful surprise, Murcer, having waged a fight against a brain tumor, showed up in the Yankee broadcast booth. They flashed his image on the big screen in right. I got a lump in my throat and let out a hearty "Bobbbbby!"

The last game I went to at the Stadium was the 2008 Old Timers' Day. It was great to see all the players I grew up with on the field at the Stadium one last time. Murcer's uniform top was hung on a wall in the dugout. The image of that flashed on the screen, and one final time, I said good-bye.

HANK WADDLES

In August of 1997, a friend's wedding brought me from California to the East Coast, and as fate would have it, Don Mattingly Day was scheduled while I was in the area.

Mattingly, for me, was everything, a bright light in a dark time. The previous generation of Yankee fans had Bobby Murcer to guide them through the wilderness, but Mattingly was better; in my teenage mind, he was legendary. I was fourteen years old when he outlasted Dave Winfield for the American League batting title, and I remember tracking each of his hits in a computer program I'd written. (This was long before the instant gratification of the Internet, and I couldn't wait for the stats in the Sunday sports section.) A few years later, just before he was robbed of what should've been his second MVP award, I announced to my mother that I would one day name my son after him. (I didn't, but I was wearing a Yankee jersey in the delivery room when my son Henry was born.) Even when I got to college I mirrored Mattingly's batting stance during intramural softball games, crouching low and turning my front toe back towards home plate.

Once, when I was nineteen or twenty, I stood five feet away from him before a game at Anaheim Stadium as he took swing after swing, pounding balls off a tee and into a net behind home plate. I couldn't bring myself to speak to him, but a young kid called out fearlessly: "Hey, Don, are you gonna hit thirty homers this year?" Without looking up from his preparation, he shot a question right back: "What if I drive in a hundred and ten? Wouldn't that be just as good?"

Moments later the players started coming off the field as their pre-game workout came to an end. An older man with a thick New York accent stood up above the dugout and pointed at Mattingly while scolding the rest of the Yankees: "Look at him! He's the only great Yankee without a ring! You get him a ring! You do what it takes to get him a ring!!" He spoke for all of us.

When I got to Manhattan on the morning of the game, I mentioned to someone that I was headed out to the Stadium that afternoon and wondered if I'd have any trouble getting a ticket. "Oh, fuhgeddaboudit!" The game had been sold out for weeks.

Undaunted, I hopped on the 4 train along with hundreds of other fans and headed up to the park. I struck up a conversation with a guy who was taking his family to the game, and at one point he asked me if I knew who Peyton Manning was. Manning was about to begin his senior year at Tennessee, and even though he was still a decade from being the ubiquitous TV pitchman that he is today, he was still the most well-known college football player in America. "Look over there. We're taking his little brother with us to the game today. He's a quarterback too." And there stood a fourteen-year-old Eli Manning, looking like any other fourteen-year-old would look—long and gangly, distracted and bored.

When you take the uptown 4 train to the Stadium, the arrival is dramatic. After rocking along underground the entire length of Manhattan, the train bursts above ground into daylight as if rising to take a much-needed breath. Almost immediately you're upon the Stadium, and if you watch closely you get a quick glimpse of the field through an opening above the bleachers. The train was full of people on their way to the game, some of them season ticket holders, others coming for the first time, but we all reacted the same way—with eyes blinking against the sudden light, we bent to look out the subway windows and pointed in unison as if to remind each other of our shared destination.

I bought a ticket from a guy on the corner, walked into the Stadium on the first-base side, and was immediately overwhelmed. The frieze encircling the outfield, the short porch in right, the black seats in center, and—best of all—a crowd filled with Yankee jerseys and caps. I stood for a moment with a lump in my throat, taking everything in. Three thousand miles from where I lived, I felt like I was home.

I made my way to my seat and watched a ceremony for Mattingly that was everything I hoped it would be. there were gifts from the team, telegrams from legends like DiMaggio and Rizzuto, and—to Mattingly's surprise—a plaque unveiled in Monument Park. But here's the moment I'll always remember. At some point during the festivities a convertible drove around the warning track with Mattingly perched upon the backseat, circling the stadium for one final ovation. I stood with fifty thousand others, chanting over and over again, "Don-ee Base-Ball!! Don-ee Base-Ball!!" and I arrived at something true.

I have never been a religious person, but this was as close to an epiphany as I have ever come. I thought of all the caps I had bought, the baseball cards I had collected, the statistics I'd memorized, and the box scores I'd pored over, and one thing became clear—throughout the course of my life, as I moved from state to state and from one group of friends to another, there had really been only one constant aside from my family: the New York Yankees. As the chants echoed back and forth across the Stadium, tears welled in my eyes and I yelled myself hoarse.

JAY JAFFE

In the course of attending approximately 130 games at Yankee Stadium II over the past thirteen years—and having spent the past eight seasons documenting my time at the ballpark via my *Futility Infielder* Web site, I've come to appreciate the park's spartan pleasures. I love the way it contains the famous reminders of its history—Monument Park, the white frieze, the flagpole in what used to be the center field patrolled by DiMaggio and Mantle, with the park's original dimensions preserved by the wall behind it, the black batter's eye where only the chosen few have reached with their towering blasts—and the portents of its own obsolescence, the narrow concourses, meager amenities, and fatal lack of luxury boxes. As limiting as that latter set is, it's also been part of the park's charm. If you go to Yankee Stadium, you're there to see a ball game, nothing more and nothing less. No fountains, waterfalls, kiddie pools, mascots, slides, or other diversions. Compared to the modern mallparks, the center field public address system is much less intrusive, even when the hated "Cotton-Eyed Joe" blares.

There are a flood of memories, including the shot Country Joe Oliver hit into the black seats in center field off none other than Greg Maddux back in 2001 during a rare Sunday night game against the Braves: or the night of August 8, 2000, when Oakland closer Jason Isringhausen came on to protect a 3–2 lead in the ninth inning but lasted only two pitches, surrendering solo homers to Bernie Williams and David Justice; or when my roommate, Issa, botched a foul ball that was headed right into his lap (with a grimace and a shrug, he slumped back into his seat as what felt like the entire crowd of 41,000 fans showered him with boos); or the pair of nights where Alex Rodriguez showed himself as inarguably the best ballplayer in the world, crushing three homers off the Angels' Bartolo Colon in the first four innings on April 26, 2005, and homering twice in one inning against the Mariners on September 5, 2007.

I will not soon forget the eerie glow the stadium produced in the distance on the night of October 30, 2001, prior to Game 3 of the World Series against the Diamondbacks. With President George W. Bush in attendance to throw out the first pitch, security was so tight that the 4 train was forced to let its passengers off one stop early, at 149th Street, and I joined the fans on a surreal pilgrimage to the radiant Mecca of baseball.

The grounds outside the Stadium were teeming with fans unable to gain immediate entry due to heightened security, and it wasn't until the second inning that I received my minia-ture American flag and ascended the stairs to a spot in the Tier Reserved section high above home plate. Before I could sit down, I was greeted by the perfect crack of the bat as Jorge Posada crushed a solo homer for the game's first run. I joined the cheer as I found my seat, thrusting my flag in the air: "Hip hip, JORGE! Hip hip, JORGE!" By that point, Bush had exited the park, and a few innings later, we watched as two Secret Service sharpshooters who had been stationed atop the stadium ported long duffel bags of rifles and telescopes past the crowd.

In the end, as I rummage through the weird and wonderful things I've witnessed firsthand at Yankee Stadium, I find only one memory which can top this list: the 1999 World Series clincher. That year, Roger Clemens was the new kid on the block, having joined the Yanks in a controversial trade for David Wells which shook up the defending champions as they opened spring training with the pressure to follow up the previous year's 125-win juggernaut.

I'd jeered the Rocket several times that season as he put up a fat 4.60 ERA to go with his meager fourteen wins, and scorned him as he'd been pounded at Fenway Park during the American League Championship Series. But on this night, with the Yanks up 3–0 in games against the Atlanta Braves, the Rocket's first World Series ring was within his grasp, and he performed his job with a zeal that stoked the sizable contingent of fans who mocked the Braves with broom-wielding tomahawk cheers.

Clemens pitched 7 ⅔ innings and left with a 3–0 lead and two men on, and when Joe Torre pulled him, Yankee Stadium shook. The entire upper deck perceptibly bounced, and I wondered about structural integrity as my friend Nick, Issa, and I—this was the only year we expanded our flex plan beyond two seats—hoisted the oversized, $10 plastic souvenir mugs of beer I had secured at last call in the top of the seventh. The stadium didn't stop shaking for the next hour and a half, as Mariano Rivera extricated the Yanks from the jam that Clemens had begun and that Jeff Nelson had exacerbated. Jim Leyritz homered in the bottom of the inning—the last home run of the 1900s, as it turns out—and the Yankees closed the deal in the top of the ninth. As Keith Lockhart's fly ball settled into Chad Curtis's glove, suddenly 56,782 people were piling on each other and cheering, then singing "New York, New York" in unison at the top of their lungs.

That was the last of sixteen World Championship ever clinched at the venerable Yankee Stadium, and for whatever reservations I may have going forward, the honor of being a part not only of that moment of baseball history but of that enormous crowd, united in such a moment of unbridled joy, is one I will never forget.

STEVEN GOLDMAN

I have a close friend—call him Jake—who is like a brother to me. When we were kids, we bonded over our mutual love of the game. His dream was always to work in the Yankees' front office. Mine was to write, though not necessarily about baseball. After many years of hard work and perseverance, he got what he wanted and became a Yankees executive. I got what I wanted too, and in fact I owe the very fact that you're reading about this to him. I was in my twenties, writing pretty much anything I could—movie reviews, screenplays, a novel, the bare bones of what would become a biography of Casey Stengel, Internet greeting cards—when Jake took an early version of the Stengel book and put it in front of people in the industry who could help me get more work writing about baseball. There began the long road that led to *Forging Genius*, *The Pinstriped Bible*, *Baseball Prospectus*, and the tiny patch of notoriety that I now enjoy. I owe Jake everything.

I would have loved, would still love, to pay him back in kind, but there was little I could do to help Jake out with the central dilemma of his career, which was that working for the Yankees proved to be a nightmare. He had a dictatorial and unsympathetic boss (George Steinbrenner was just a profane, disembodied voice on the phone from Tampa and not at all a

part of the daily life of the team), and a fluctuating job description that really didn't engage him emotionally or intellectually
and had little to do with his credentials. He had many experiences there that were patently surreal, reaching a level of absur-
dity that when people would ask me if the depiction of life
with the Yankees on *Seinfeld* was accurate, I'd say, in complete
seriousness, "No. Too tame."

Jake spent many days feeling isolated, both because of
the constant abuse from his boss and the constant turnover
in almost every department. And then there was the physical
location of his office. You have to imagine Jake, marooned on
the Mechanical Level of the Stadium, a desolate, windowless,
undecorated place of exposed wiring and dangling insulation,
busted seats, and old vending carts. That's where the Yankees
had about half their offices—the original ballpark wasn't built
to house the full Yankees operation, but when Steinbrenner
bought the club he closed their midtown offices and brought
all the executives to the Bronx, whether there was room for
them or not. Jake sat there, day after day, often more than
sixteen hours a day. His boss decreed that though he had no
responsibilities relating to stadium operations, Jake had to
be at work both during regular business hours and all home
games—miserable. He desperately wanted to leave, but how
do you quit on your dream?

It was towards the end of Jake's time with the Yankees that
I made one of many visits, probably to do some research for
an article for *Yankees Magazine*. After I had done my work in
the unlit, unventilated room that then held the Yankees media
archive, I repaired to Jake's office. Somewhere below us, a
ballgame was going on. We could hear it but not see it. He
was inconsolably depressed. I don't remember what we talked
about after he pointed out that I was now covered in sweat,

dust, and cobwebs and desperately needed a new shirt, but I'm certain it involved his career prospects. The mood grew darker. He stood up abruptly, a mischievous gleam in his eyes. "Come with me. There's something I've been wanting to show you."

I followed him down the long, narrow corridor that makes up the office portion of the Mechanical Level to a locked door. He opened it. We stepped into a cavernous area, dimly lit by widely spaced safety lights. I could not perceive the ceiling—the space extended upwards into dark infinity. There was a wall hard to my right and another wall that began far to my left, then sloped sharply towards us, rising up into the darkness. The floor too had vanished, replaced by a fire engine red metal catwalk that bounced when we walked on it. The Stadium crowd was incredibly loud here, as if we were among them, and it quickly dawned on me that they were both below and above us—we were inside the upper deck.

We moved down the catwalk. I could see that we were just a foot or so above the drop ceiling above the loge boxes. The tiles, weighed down with sandbags, were imperfectly placed, and you could see thin lines of light from below, and even make out the shifting masses of people. A Yankee made a hit. The noise level rose. The catwalk seemed to sway in response to the crowd. I started to get very nervous—if this thing gave way we would be landing in their laps—at best. "Let's go," I urged Jake, but he was still bouncing down the catwalk.

"After that beam fell, they gutted out this whole area and put these things in. I don't think anyone has been back here except the engineers. They're pretty sure it will all hold together. What are you worried about?"

At intervals, the pathway sprouted additional catwalks, perpendicular to the main trunk. These extended all the way to the far wall. Jake walked out on one of these. I winced, watching him make what seemed like a tightrope walk out over the crowd.

"It just doesn't seem that stable to me."

Despite being on a catwalk, Jake was no cat, not in agility or weight, and though he had been in a somber mood for months or years at this point, he was suddenly giddy, even manic. "It's fine!" he shouted. "Look!" He began hopping, springing off the catwalk like it was a mattress. "Come on!"

I have since discussed these events with Jake, and he insists that he was completely in his right mind at this moment and that he was simply trying to give me a look at a part of the Stadium that the public never sees. Perhaps, but I thought: "My god, he's finally lost it. He can't bring himself to quit, so he's trying to kill himself . . . or get fired for breaking the Stadium." Another Yankee made a hit. The catwalk went left and right. Jake, still hopping, went up and down. My stomach was trying to follow them both. I made a decision: time to go. I turned on my heels and made a beeline for the door. "Hey!" Jake shouted, but I could hear him rattling up the catwalk behind me. We made it through the door. Safe. No headlines about fat men falling through the ceilings.

I don't remember much else about that night, don't know if the Yankees lost or won. I just remember a feeling of dread for Jake. I was both right and wrong, right in that it would have been better for him to have left sooner than he did, more than a couple of seasons later, wrong to feel dread; he bounced back just fine, though I know he has some resentments about the experience that can never be unmade.

Since then, in my professional capacity, I've had some great experiences at the Stadium. I've had one-on-one moments with greats of the game in the dugouts and the clubhouses, and I especially cherish those conversations that proved to be last chances, like those with Enos Slaughter, Hank Bauer, Bobby Murcer, and others. In giving me those memories the Stadium has more than made up for the numerous losses pitched by Tim Leary, Greg Cadaret, and Bob Shirley that I paid to witness. Yet, for all of that, when I think of the Stadium after it's gone, it will be of my friend, tie flapping as he jumped on a secret catwalk, trying to leap clear of the one thing he had always wanted and had had the misfortune to get.

JON DeROSA

On January 22, 1982, Reggie Jackson signed with the California Angels. It was the latest in a series of difficult lessons for me—a six-year-old who otherwise had it pretty good. In rapid succession, Darth Vader revealed he was Luke Skywalker's father, the Yankees crashed out of the only two baseball seasons I had ever followed, and my grandmother passed days after my little brother was born on my sixth birthday. I was looking for a fight and George Steinbrenner and his Yankees were in the wrong place at the wrong time.

I assigned Steinbrenner and Vader to the same category of evil: each had reached into my life and changed things forever. I actively rooted for the Yankees' decline the way I rooted for the fall of the Empire. I removed my Yankee baseball cards from the binder, secured them with merciless rubber bands and tossed them in with obscure Seattle Mariners, Cleveland, Indians and other total strangers. From that point on, I rooted for the Angels.

In 1982, for a kid in New York, that was difficult. You had to *write a letter* to the team, addressed to the stadium itself, requesting them to *mail you an order form* so that you might have the opportunity to buy something with a halo on it. My mother wrote such a letter and, by the grace of Gene Autry, was allowed to purchase a cap, a helmet, a jersey, and for some reason, Angels wristbands.

I wore the whole ensemble to Yankee Stadium on Tuesday April 27th, 1982, Reggie's first game back in New York. My father and older brother were with me but I was scared stiff. What if he struck out? What if they booed? What if the Yankees were right?

We watched batting practice from right field in a light rain as a buzzing crowd filed in around us. Our seats were in the upper deck between first base and right field, where we munched on hot dogs. I felt grown-up whenever I was allowed to get two, but that night, my nervous stomach wasn't accommodating. The rain made the bun on the second hot dog a little soggy.

When Reggie came to bat in the second inning, Bob Sheppard announced his name with such elegance that I imagined it was a personal statement, "I should be announcing this name every night." This was the moment I dreaded. Would they boo? The crowd stood and chanted: REG-GIE, REG-GIE, REG-GIE. Buoyed by the warmth of the welcome, I got to my feet, but my jaw was frozen shut and I couldn't move my lips. My dad put his arm around me as Ron Guidry poured in a heater. Reggie took his massive cut, but he got jammed and popped out. I was back in my seat the instant I saw Reggie's reaction.

The game rolled along at a pace more akin to a 100-meter dash than a modern American League baseball game—they got through seven innings in one hour and 51 minutes before the game was called due to rain. When Reggie batted in the fifth, the crowd rose for him again. REG-GIE, REG-GIE, REG-GIE. He yanked a single to right field and was rewarded with brief applause. I was silent throughout this at-bat, too, but the base hit calmed my nerves temporarily. The crowd asked; Reggie delivered. Contract complete, customers satisfied, right? Even a child should have known better. Yankee fans didn't ask—they demanded. And they didn't want a single; they wanted a home run.

When they greeted Reggie with his chant for the third time in the seventh, my stomach knotted, and I wished they would stop chanting. It wasn't fanatical devotion; it was the begging of spoiled children. REG-GIE, REG-GIE, REG-GIE might as well have been MORE, MORE, MORE. I knew it was not fair to ask for so much. In this world I was learning about, teams lose, people die; things just don't usually work out . . .

I saw Reggie's black bat whip through the hitting zone; the ball accelerated at an improbable speed and angle at impact and assumed a trajectory that could have sent it across the street if not for the upper deck façade. As the ball sped past my face it erased all my doubts and fears and I felt a lightness rise from my gut to my head. Pure relief. I couldn't hear anything because my mind had not yet validated this moment as reality. Then the noise just materialized in my ears: REG-GIE, REG-GIE, REG-GIE, louder than the other three times combined. My brother and father jostled me from side to side as they chanted along.

I stayed quiet. How did this happen? Did I use the Force to will that ball out of the park? I couldn't even comprehend that I just got exactly what I wanted. What were the ramifications of getting what you pray for? I should have been screaming my head off, but I just stared out at Reggie rounding the bases, making sure he touched every one and hoping he was as happy as I was.

The chanting didn't end when Reggie reached the dugout. When he came out for his curtain call, as if they had rehearsed it prior to the game, the crowd turned toward Steinbrenner's box and let him have it. Steinbrenner SUCKS, Steinbrenner

SUCKS, Steinbrenner SUCKS! All of the emotion that had built up in my little body flowed through the crowd into the damp Stadium air. My brother and father were gleefully singing the song, rousing me to participate. But I felt bad for George and I kept silent.

JONAH KERI

I was eight years old in the summer of 1983, traveling from Montreal with my grandparents to visit my ultra-religious relatives in Brooklyn. It was a shock, sitting there on a Saturday—no TV, no activity, nothing to do but stare at the walls. The next day would be better, though. Field trip to the Statue of Liberty, all kinds of neat stuff for a kid. And on Monday . . . Yankee Stadium! *The* Yankee Stadium! I could hardly wait.

When we got back from our Sunday of sightseeing, I peppered my grandfather with questions. How would we be getting to the game? (By subway, cool!) Where were we sitting? (We didn't have tickets yet, but there were plenty available . . . hopefully upper deck, where foul balls glided in softly.) Who were they playing again? (The Red Sox, sweet!)

I woke up early the next day. I could barely sleep with all the excitement of the game ahead. We'd hop on the train around 12:30 and make our way up to the Bronx, plenty of time for a rare weekday 2 PM start time, I was told.

Then the morning started getting hotter. And hotter. By eleven the temperature had spiked above 90 degrees, with stifling humidity. Not that it bothered me. All I could think about was going to the Stadium to see the game. My grandfather had other ideas.

Me: "So when are we going?"

Papa: "I don't think we can go, it's too hot."

Me: "What?! I thought you said we were going!"

Papa: "I'm sorry Jonah, it's just too hot outside. You can listen to the game here, on the radio."

My little heart was broken. Deep down, I knew my Papa would've done anything for me. He always did. But at that moment, I wanted to cry. With no TV around, I settled in on the couch of that Brooklyn walk-up to listen to the game I so badly wanted to see in person.

Both teams stayed scoreless through the first four innings. Then the Yankees scored once each in the fifth and sixth, the second run coming on a long home run by Don Baylor (I was a precocious fan, I knew Baylor was the big guy with the straight-up batting stance).

The Red Sox still couldn't push across a run. Something odd was going on, though. I noticed, about four innings in, that they also didn't have a hit. They still didn't after six innings, the likes of Wade Boggs, Jim Rice, and Dwight Evans all shut down by the Yankee pitcher.

The game moved along, and still no hits for Boston. As they came up to bat in the eighth, it dawned on me: Is it possible that I may end up missing a no-hitter?! One-two-three went Evans, Nichols, and Stapleton. The Yankees scored two more in the bottom of the eighth, bringing their flawless lefty back to the mound for the ninth.

I didn't want this to happen. Even at eight years old, I knew how awful it would be if I came that close to seeing a no-hitter—against the Red Sox!—at Yankee Stadium!!!—only to miss it.

Newman drew a leadoff walk. OK, good, the pitcher's getting tired, the Sox are going to rally. I didn't much care who won, just please, no no-hitter. But then Hoffman grounded out. So did Remy. One batter remained.

That batter was Boggs. In just his second season, he was at the height of his powers, destined to hit .361 that year. He'd gone 0 for 3 to that point in the game. He was due.

Or so I thought. The pitcher got two strikes on him. PLEASE WADE, GET A HIT! The pitcher rocked back, fired . . . and struck him out. I had just missed a no-hitter. Yankees–Red Sox. Yankee Stadium. ON THE FOURTH OF JULY!

To this day, twenty-five years later, I still make sure never to break plans to go to the ballpark. To this day, I cringe whenever I see a game on July Fourth, knowing that on the scoreboard they'll flash a graphic for "This Day in History", reminding me of the masterpiece I missed.

To this day, I curse the name of Dave Righetti.

ROB NEYER

I almost missed it. Yankee Stadium. *Sunday Night Baseball* on ESPN. Roger Clemens vs. Pedro Martinez. And I almost missed it. The beginning, anyway. I was in Manhattan that afternoon, and took the 6 train to the Bronx. As you might know but I didn't, the 6 doesn't stop at Yankee Stadium, but instead blows right on past. By the time I realized what I'd done, I was three stops past the Stadium and wound up somewhere called Cypress Avenue, which felt like a long, long way from Ruth's House.

I did get back in time, a couple of minutes before eight; because the game was on ESPN, it wouldn't start until 8:05. Still, I had no idea where I was going; Section 11? Box 41? Row C? An usher guided me toward the infield, and eventually I realized where I would be sitting: fourth row, right behind the Yankees' dugout. Nirvana.

There I joined Andy, a Harvard law student who had so graciously offered me the ticket. At that moment, settling into my incredible seat for a night game featuring two of baseball's best teams—ancient foes no less—and two Hall of Fame starting pitchers, the game was already one of the more memorable in my life.

Through the first eight innings, how many runners reached base? One. With one out in the seventh, Trot Nixon tripled to left center. The Yankee infielders moved in—a single run might be quite precious—but Clemens didn't need any help, striking out Brian Daubach (looking) and Nomar Garciaparra (swinging). That half-inning aside, there was little sustained drama involving the hitters in more than a bystanding way (Pedro struck out nine batters in the game, Clemens thirteen).

What happened in the ninth inning could almost as easily have happened in the seventh inning, or the eighth. But it happened in the ninth, thus lifting tonight's proceedings from good game to man, what a great game.

John Valentin led off for the Sox and tapped a grounder to second baseman Chuck Knoblauch. One out. Jason Varitek tried to bunt his way on, but he didn't get the ball close enough to the third-base line and Clemens threw him out. Two outs, and it's getting late, and we're starting to wonder if this one's going past midnight.

But then Clemens ran a pitch high and inside to Jeff Frye, who dropped his bat and trotted down to first base . . . But no! Plate umpire Brian Runge is waving off the HBP, then pointing madly at Frye's bat on the ground, telling all of us that before the ball struck Frye, it struck his bat. Foul ball. Frye argued and Jimy Williams argued, but there was nothing to be done about it.

Frye meted out the best kind of justice, though, smashing a hot grounder right back up the middle. Clemens could have made the play, maybe should have made the play. But he did not make the play. Sometimes these fractions of inches become important, and these fractions became terribly important a moment later because Trot Nixon batted next. And Nixon creamed one of the Rocket's rockets well into the right-field stands. Two-zip, Red Sox. (Later, we learned that after Nixon struck out looking in the first inning, Clemens had screamed at him, "Swing the bat!")

Knoblauch led off the bottom of the ninth, and Pedro nailed him. Was it a coincidence that, just a few moments earlier, Clemens had come inside on Jeff Frye? Does Pedro have so much confidence that he'd happily award the Yankees a baserunner in the ninth inning of a 2–0 game? Nah, I don't think so. I think the ball just got away from him. And Knoblauch's the sort of guy who probably enjoyed getting plunked. That brought up Jeter, who promptly singled to right field, Knoblauch stopping at second.

Out of the Red Sox dugout popped Jimy Williams, and I was so sure about what would happen next that, on my scorecard, I drew the line that denotes a pitching change. I had no good idea of Pedro's pitch count, but I estimated somewhere around 100, given that he'd run very few deep counts, and had faced only twenty-eight batters to that point. He'd been a bit shaky lately, though, if Tino Martinez's long fly in the seventh and Ricky Ledee's longer fly in the eighth were any indication. What the Sox really needed was a double play, and Derek Lowe—ready to come in at a moment's notice—throws a heavy sinker that results in a lot of double plays.

Say what you want about him, but Jimy Williams is his own man. After a lengthy consultation with his battery, Williams shuffled back to his subterranean lair, never having made any gesture toward his bullpen. It would be Pedro's game, and he responded by striking out Paul O'Neill with high heat. Next up: Bernie Williams, and he shot a fly ball into the right-field corner. Initially I thought it was gone, and part of me wanted it to be gone. Yeah, I was pulling for the Red Sox, but what a thing to see, a game-winning, three-run bomb that would have turned the Stadium into the Happiest Place on Earth. But Nixon flagged down the ball near the warning track; Knoblauch tagged at second and went to third.

That brought up Jorge Posada, and he missed Pedro's first two pitches by a couple of feet. One change up and it's over, right? Ah, but this game wasn't prescribed. Posada took a ball. And then, impossibly, Pedro plunked him, too.

So here comes Tino Martinez with the bases loaded. A single probably ties the game, a double probably wins it, and a home run gets you the biggest celebration in the Bronx since last October. By this point I was hoping for an out, or a home run. This game, it seemed to me, should be decided by the two starting pitchers. Plus, I was drained. After being on edge for nearly nine full innings, Bernie's drive to the track had grabbed most of what emotional energy I had left.

I'll be honest with you: I'm not in love with Yankee Stadium. Fenway Park is a place. The Green Monster and Pesky's Pole and Lansdowne Street and all the rest. If a native of Alpha Centauri 4 came to Sol 3 for the express purpose of watching a couple of baseball games but knew nothing of the game's lore, Yankee Stadium would be just another ballpark (granted, a large and fairly rowdy one). Take our alien to Fenway Park, though, and he'd likely fall in love with not only the building, but the game on the field as well.

There is one thing that I do love about Yankee Stadium, though, and it's probably not something you would guess.

I love the clock.

At the top of the scoreboard that's just to the left of straightaway center field, you can always find the time. And not just any old time, but the OFFICIAL TIME.

The time of my life runs according to the baseball season, especially this particular baseball season. So there's the

OFFICIAL TIME in big block letters, my official time, always available in one's field of vision, just like the pitcher and the batter. And at 11:08 tonight, a game I'll never forget officially ended when Tino Martinez chopped a routine grounder to second baseman Jeff Frye, who made the routine throw to first base. At 11:08 tonight, I was as happy to love this sport as I have ever been.

NATHAN WARD

As a Boston fan behind enemy lines, over the years I've seen some profiles in courage: Jim Rice climbing into the third base seats to retrieve his Lucky Gamer hat grabbed by a fan after an on-field collision; the Sox outfielders staring in through a gunpowder haze during a Monday night Game of the Week unwisely scheduled for July 2, 1979. I've seen Pedro and Clemens lock up in a testy (2–0) classic. I was even there when Bob Sheppard intoned that the oft-fired manager Billy Martin would return for more punishment as skipper the following season—the crowd went wild. But my favorite Stadium moment doesn't involve a Yankee or Sox player at all.

The summer of 1978, Bobby Bonds, the talented but bridge-burning father of Barry, had just gone from the White Sox to Texas, and would pull up stakes five times in four years. When his Rangers came to New York, my father and grandfather took me for an outing in the Bronx.

We sat way up, well to the right of home plate. It seemed improbable country for a ball to land, but at the railing in front of us were a father and two young boys who'd brought their short rubbery mitts, as if a foul might somehow strike a whippy enough current to detour our way. Batting righty, Bonds cut under a pitch just enough to do exactly that—send it spinning upward all the way to our section, just clearing the heads of the two young sentries at the rail.

My grandfather was then in his late sixties, a boyhood Cleveland fan who'd adopted the White Sox during his years with the University of Chicago. But like the small boys in front of him and the younger men he'd brought to the game, he had never caught a foul ball. This despite the hundreds of games he'd attended, seeing his hero George Sisler with his menacing black bat and stubbly visage and the young Willie Mays, whose hat flew off as Grandpa watched him round second.

To his left was my father, then in his late thirties, a fan of almost any fight, but whose baseball season really began once the 162-game preliminaries were over. And to his left was his own fifteen-year-old son, bravely clutching my Sox hat rather than attract more flying spit from the Bronx boys. As the Bonds ball just cleared the two youngsters before us, they waved their gloves like shipwrecked kids at a passing airplane, then it came for me.

My father deeply regrets what happened next, but my grandfather, who took a much longer view, never did. With the ball spinning toward my head, my father instinctively shielded his boy's eyes with his hands, blinding me but allowing the ball to clip my still-raised palm and bounce perfectly into the soft-handed embrace of my grandfather. There was silence through much of our side of the Stadium, and pleading puppy eyes from the boys in front as well as from their dad. But my grandfather stood firm and looked away, holding the ball up to show the crowd the treasure was safe: Over the big roar he loudly explained, "I've waited all my life to catch one of those." Then, for the front row's benefit, he added, "I'm giving it to my grandson." Although over time it did gain some green scuffs from our occasional games of catch, the ball lived mostly at the bottom of his closet.

More recently, I dropped another one at the Stadium, sitting high up toward the end of a Sox-Yankee game. Manny was fouling them off against Mariano when he sent one scudding up toward me—it looked so weirdly low as it spun that I had my hands out of place and it careened off my thumb. Manny hit the next pitch out, prompting the Yankee guys behind me to slap my shoulder, "You shoulda caught that! You *&$#ed the whole karma of the game!"

If, in some small way, my incompetence as a fielder finally helped my team, then I am glad. But, considering how long my grandfather waited for his first and only chance, with assists from two other generations of his family, I don't deserve another for a long time.

DAYN PERRY

When I was in second grade I read about a girl named Frieda. She lived in New York City, which I had heard of but could scarcely imagine, as it was far away from the small Mississippi town where I grew up. New York was big and famous and full of hard mysteries. Frieda rode the subway. She played double-dutch on sidewalks. She sat on stoops and bought milk for her mother at the bodega on the corner. It snowed there.

Maybe it was that same day when I got home from school or maybe it was another day, but I dragged down the "N" volume of our World Book Encyclopedia and looked up Frieda's hometown. Inside was a foldout map. That map was sinewed with roads, train lines, expressways, and side streets. The way the mapped look, so busy and twined and clotted, I could compare it only to . . . the entrails of fish?

It was just a map, but like any good map it hinted at the real place behind it. The names on it beckoned. And those names in and around New York were like nothing I'd ever heard—arresting in their tough sounds and, I imagined, the tough places they evoked. Hoboken. Brooklyn. Bayonne. The Meatpacking District. Canarsie. Nyack. Red Hook. Hell's Kitchen. Pelham Bay Park. Bensonhurst. Throgs Neck. And then: The Bronx.

I think—and I really do think this—that I've been a fool for New York ever since I first ran across the word "Bronx." It was a word perfect in its ugliness, the toughest word. Bronx. And what kind of place had "the" in front of it? Whatever it was, there could only be one.

I knew from watching *Monday Night Baseball*, from the box scores in the *Mississippi Press* and from my 1979 Topps cards that the Yankees played in Frieda's New York, but it wasn't until I was older that I learned they played in the Bronx. I thought differently of them—better of them, I guess—when I found that out. They would never be my favorite team, but thanks to my child's grasp of the world—and of that word—there will always be something at once classic and menacing and worlds away about the team from the Bronx.

I was nineteen years old when I finally made it to New York City. And I was thirty when I finally made it to Yankee Stadium and the Bronx. I was apartment-sitting for a friend and his wife in Queens—not as good of a word—and I made my way to the 4 train and rode it to the 161st Street stop.

It was an afternoon of connoisseur's baseball. Mike Mussina struck out ten, but the Tigers, a terrible team that summer, pushed across a run in the eighth and went on to win, 2–1. I barely noticed.

There is a difference between looking at something and watching something. You look at a painting. You look at a dead animal. But you watch a ball game. You watch the Bronx. So I watched the people around me, and I watched what I could see of the city—of the Bronx—beyond the white, scalloped arches that crowned the park. You see, when I'm there, I walk around in a fugue, as though I've been allowed to relive a memory. It's a place I still lurch to imagine.

SCOTT RAAB

I was born and bred in Cleveland, Ohio, and I've loathed the New York Yankees and everything they stand for—arrogance, entitlement, and money-worship—for as long as I can recall. Even past the point where I realized that I myself was a smug, spoiled, money-grubbing New York–area-dwelling media hack, I hated the hulking, brutish Yankees.

Yankee Stadium? I'd rather pass a gallstone than put a single penny in any Steinbrenner's pocket. Sure, I'd been there a few times, those memories frosted over by decades of heavy self-medication. My highlight House-That-Blah-Blah-Built memory was watching on TV when last year's Tribe clinched the LDS at Yankee Stadium. In that storied house. With Bayonne Joe Borowski, no less, on the hill. Sweet almost beyond words, and I cried like a baby to see the dogpile at the end, then went upstairs to wake up my nine-year-old son and start spreading the news.

He hates the Yankees, too. But like me, he loves baseball, so last Sunday we went to see a ball game, and to pay homage. Because you can love baseball and hate the Yankees, but you can't walk into Yankee Stadium with a hard heart—not if you're a baseball fan. We weren't paying homage to the pinstripes or our bile; we were there to honor eighty-five years of history, eat some hot dogs, and unwind at a beautiful, battered ballyard.

Who knows what a kid remembers? Hell, I seem to remember admiring Mickey Mantle once upon a time. My boy loved every minute. And so did I. It was hot, brutally hot, so we had to suck it up and buy a couple of Yankees caps—$50 that will surely help sign Grady Sizemore one sorry day—and the upper-deck concession stands ran out of ice by the sixth inning, and yeah, the Yankees won. No problem. A-Rod belted a grand slam, Cano got yanked for dogging it, and Jeter tied Lou Gehrig's record for hits at Yankee Stadium: great ball game. Great game.

We gave away the caps on the subway home, but I'll hold on to the day for a long time—and to old, doomed Yankee Stadium. I don't know about redemption, and like Woody Allen, old Clevelanders don't mellow—we ripen and rot. I had an epiphany once: In real life, there ain't no epiphanies. I don't want miracles, much less expect 'em. I took my son to see the Yankees play at Yankee Stadium. That's close enough for me.

JOHN C. McGINLEY

I'm spitballing with you but my favorite memories of Yankee Stadium came from a period of time when everyone I knew was an unemployed actor. I'm from New York originally. I was born in St Vincent's in the Village and lived in Peter Stuyvesant Town until I was ten. Then my parents moved to the suburbs in Jersey but later I went to NYU and then lived on Perry and Bleecker for close to twenty years before I finally came out here in '91. I got out of NYC in '84 and for the next five years, everyone I knew was unemployed actors. You'd get an off-Broadway play, or a day job on a soap, but mostly it was a grind. It was a struggle.

I loved to go up to the Bronx on an afternoon and catch a game. I'd go up to a day game at 161st and find all the other unemployed actors. Some guys would go to Shea but I never rooted for the Mets until Willie became their manager a few years ago and then I *loved* them.

The Yankees were terrible then. It wasn't like today, getting a ticket was no sweat even if you were dead broke. Seats weren't hard to come by. If a scalper was eating a sandwich two innings into the game, you could get in on the cheap. The scalper would have to eat it by that time. So we'd start up in the cheap seats and then move down. Most of us brought our own booze in with us, everybody brought what they needed. There would only be something like 12,000 people in the Stadium on a weekday afternoon. The ushers would let you down by the dugout because they were out-of work actors too.

The one thing that was understood was that nobody asked each other what they were doing. 'Cause the answer was, you're doing nothing. You're going to a Yankee game cause the phone's not ringing. There were no cell phones in those days so guys would get up during the game and go use a payphone to call their *machine* to see if anyone on the planet would give them a job. And then you'd go back and watch the game for three hours and get lost in it and be happy.

We'd bust each other's humps and argue and see who could memorize the most statistics. Tommy Sizemore had a photographic memory that was not dissimilar to Bob Costas's ability to recall stats and facts. I was so pathetic I'd bring Roger Angell books up. I read his stuff in the *New Yorker* and his collections. Halberstam's writing in the *Summer of '49* and especially *The Teammates*. I'm a sucker for baseball writing because the game lends itself to poetic prose. Some people think it's too much but I think it's great. So we'd talk about baseball and be having a good time.

I loved Yankee Stadium because of the colors and the smells and the potential for anything to happen in the bottom of the ninth. Baseball dictates that you can always come back and even in those years when the team was awful anything could happen. It was the perfect place to be for a young, unemployed actor. Things just seemed unlimited. Day games are from God.

(As told to Alex Belth)

LUIS GUZMAN

I grew up in Greenwich Village in the sixties on Tenth and Hudson. I went to PS 41. Then when I was ten, we moved to the LES, to the Lower East Side. All my life I've been a Yankee fan. I remember Horace Clarke, Kekich, Peterson, Hamilton, "the Folly Floater." When I was between the ages of say ten and fourteen which, would have been '66 to '70, I'd get together with my buddies in the Village: my man Wayne Teagarden, my boy Norman sometimes too, and we'd shine shoes outside of the bank of Seventh Avenue and Christopher Street. We'd shine shoes in the morning, make enough money, sneak on the train, get up to the Stadium, and sneak into the bleachers. We'd make $2–3, which was pretty good back then. Sometimes we'd pay to get in, it depended. It was fifty, seventy-five cents. We'd fill up on hot dogs and soda and cracker jacks, which was the thing at the time.

Back then, they had day games during the week. We used to go out Sunday for bat day and hat day and ball day and yadda-yadda day. It was great. I'd go to every Old Timers' game, that was a big thing for me, and nothing was bigger than the day Mickey Mantle retired. We had seen Mickey play, he had hit a few home runs when I was there, that was big stuff man. But that day, his family was there, it was heavy.

Between '66–'70 the Yankees weren't doing too good. But we watched Mickey Mantle wind down his career, and you'd see other guys that would come in—Yaz with the Red Sox, Luis Aparicio with the Twins, Harmon Killebrew, Rod Carew.

We didn't know at the time but the old Stadium was . . . it was amazing. They had those beams that would come down and we'd wonder how anybody would be able to see if they had to sit behind one of them. But we were always in the bleachers, the right-field bleachers, cause we used to like looking into the bullpen to see who is warming up. Remember when the bullpen was in the tunnel? We'd be talking to the pitchers.

Back then Yankee Stadium was a real relaxed, kicked-back kind of a place. They didn't have guys coming onto the field between innings like now. It wasn't this high-security place. It's when it was a ballpark. Dude, we used to wait for the third out in the top or bottom of the ninth and after the third out we'd jump over the railing and run around all over the outfield. There would be fifty, one hundred kids running around. But that's all we'd do was run around. We were respectful about it.

What ruined it were the people who would jump on the field and tear up the grass. We were just happy just running around. The Stadium guards would open up the gates to the bullpen and behind it the gates to the exit. They'd wait for us to run out of air. And then we'd exit and go home. There was no harassing. That's when it was worthwhile being a kid.

But even the renovated place had nostalgia. I was there in the seventies when they turned it around. And later, I took my first son there with me when he was one, one-and-a-half. This was in '92. We're sitting front row right on top of the visitor's dugout and who are they playing? They're playing the Toronto Blue Jays—Joe Carter, Robbie Alomar, David Cone, Devon White, all those guys. So Robbie gives my little boy a ball between innings. My boy looks at the ball, and I'm like, "Oh, my god, he just got a ball from Robbie Alomar." Little guy looks at the ball and throws it back out on the field. I said are you kidding me? Robbie gave me the ball back, he thought it was funny. He and I became buddies after that.

And Devon White, what a gentleman he was. One of the nicest guys I ever met. He goes to one of the people who takes your order and says, "Whatever he wants." And the lady goes, "Ah, I need money." I go, "Devon, Devon, don't worry about it, I got it." What does he do, he goes down to the clubhouse, comes back and gives the lady $200 and says, "Whatever he wants."

I said, "Damn, thank you."

I remember being at the game when Charlie Hayes caught the last out. I sat right behind home plate for that game. That's probably the loudest I ever heard Yankee Stadium. Mickey Mantle Day was big too, I was there when I was a kid, but I was out in the bleachers for that, when you sit in the box seats the sound is different, that's for sure. There's nothing like the World Series in the Bronx, man.

(As told to Alex Belth)

CLIFF CORCORAN

The day before the final game at Yankee Stadium, the Yankees announced that they were going to allow fans who arrived early to that game to walk the perimeter of the field, giving many the opportunity to both set foot on and say goodbye to that hallowed ground in the Bronx. The field was to be open to fans between one and four PM. Eager to take advantage of that opportunity, my wife, Becky, and I arrived at the Stadium just before one on Sunday, September 21, the day of the final game. As we walked over the pedestrian bridge, past the smokestack bat toward Gate 4 behind home plate, we saw a significant, but not overwhelming, crowd and decided that we could afford to scoot up 161st Street to grab a couple of sandwiches. As we walked by, Gate 4 was opening for the last time on a game day.

After getting our grub, we queued up at Gate 2 behind left field. The fans were going to be let onto the field via Monument Park, so we figured that entering the ballpark close to Monument Park would increase our chances of actually getting on the field. The security at Gate 2 was well organized and allowed fans to enter in large waves so as to control traffic. Becky and I entered with the third wave, no later than 1:30, and proceeded to follow the crowd past the entrance to Monument Park and up the series of ramps in the far left-field corner of the Stadium.

The line snaked around the entire upper deck, finally ending a level lower, way out in right field.

By three, we were just to the right-field side of home plate on the Tier level. At a bit before four, we were halfway down the third-base line, still on the Tier level, and word was starting to spread that the field had been closed. Uninterested in spending another two and a half hours in line on the off chance that we'd get to see Monument Park one last time, Becky and I took off for the main level to walk around the lower deck.

As we circled the Stadium, separated from our original destination on the field by the main boxes and the Stadium security who guarded the chains keeping the hoi polloi out of said boxes, Becky and I took in the beautiful late-summer day and the beloved old ballpark. Near the visitors dugout, Joe Girardi approached the fans on the field to meet, greet, and sign autographs. As we walked behind home—passing behind Jane Lang, a longtime Yankee fan from my hometown, and her seeing-eye dog Laramie—we saw some of his players doing likewise. As the fans on the field receded, it became clear just how extensive the swarm of media in front of the Yankee dugout was. I snapped a quick photo of the *Baseball Tonight* crew, who were taking a commercial break on a makeshift set, but otherwise paid the horde little mind.

After breathing the park in from the seating bowl, Becky and I attempted to make our way to our right-field bleacher seats. The bleachers were usually inaccessible from the rest of the Stadium, but we were told by a staffer that we could access them via Monument Park. Out in left field, we encountered a pair of roadblocks and were told to wait there by a female cop directing traffic while standing on a chair and blocking the sun from her face by holding her hat in her hand. After we stood in that same sun for too long, a Stadium staffer of higher authority informed us and the other bleacher-ticket holders that had assembled there that we had to go to Gate 6, back in right field, to get to our seats.

As frustrating as all of this was, it gave us an accidental tour of large swaths of the Stadium, sending us to nooks and crannies I'd never seen before and eventually through the old Yankee bullpen in right field to get to our usual Section 37. By the time we settled into our spots on the Row JJ bench (seats 5 and 6), the Yankees were on the field stretching in a circle.

Jason Giambi put on the best show in batting practice, littering the upper deck in right field with abused baseballs. A few came off his and others' bats into our section. Noted ballhawk Zack Hample lurked in the near front corner of the right-field box seats and managed to snag several balls before the Yankees departed. He then threw on an Orioles cap and a Cal Ripken T-shirt in an attempt to get more from the Baltimore players who were taking the field for BP.

With the Yankees having retreated to the clubhouse, Becky and I, finally in our seats, settled in, finished off our sandwiches, and talked about the Stadium and our day to that point. Becky enjoys going to baseball games, and at times will get even more upset about a poor play, bad decision, or distasteful opponent than I will. She had been particularly excited about the prospect of getting to go on the field, but I counseled her to expect disappointment, and was surprised at just how much it seemed to be eating at her. When I mentioned it to her, she gave me a few awkward half-answers and we changed the subject. A few minutes later we had stopped chatting and were taking in the ballpark when Becky tapped me on the leg and told me she had something to tell me.

She looked at me, beaming, almost blushing. "Guess," she said.

I don't like to leap to conclusions. I also don't like to get worked up over something until I'm sure it's going to happen, so I was afraid to assume what she wanted me to. Becky could see a hint of recognition cross my face and started nodding furiously.

"Really?"

"Uh-huh. I took a test this morning."

"And it was positive?"

"Uh-huh."

We embraced tightly, joyously, and I became flooded with emotions. I was already emotional over the significance of the day and the impending loss of a building that had come to feel like a second home to me over the preceding twenty years. Now, the day suddenly had a far greater significance. I was going to be a dad.

Becky was upset because she wanted to tell me on the field, which only made the hours-long wait in the upper deck concourses all the more excruciating for her, but she needn't have been let down. I'd been witness to a lot of great moments on the field at Yankee Stadium over the years, but nothing will ever top that moment in the bleachers on the old yard's final day. I'm disappointed that Becky and I will never be able to take our daughter to Yankee Stadium, but I can always tell her that, even if only in the most technical sense, she was there.

JOSH WILKER

I

A few months ago I saw Yankee Stadium for the last time. I was driving on the Major Deegan, headed north after a short trip back to the city where I'd lived throughout my twenties. My first impulse was to give Yankee Stadium the finger.

But then I remembered what happened the last time I gave Yankee Stadium the finger, years ago. My brother and I and another friend—call him Butch—were heading upstate for a court date. On another earlier trip of ours upstate Butch had gotten arrested for being the point man in our self-consciously absurd drunken heist scheme to steal a poster from a movie theater lobby. The poster featured an ape wearing glasses and playing chess. We were all pushing thirty by then. We had not figured anything out. Butch was apprehended by blond and tan teenagers in national-movie-theater-chain golf shirts. They held him until the cops arrived, chewing their bubble gum.

Anyway, a few weeks later we headed back upstate on the Major Deegan and passed Yankee Stadium on the way. This was during the era when the Yankees won the World Series every single year. Every single lonely-stupid-meaningless-drunken-suffering New York year. My brother and I were Red Sox fans, and Butch was a Mets fan. We all felt conquered. We all felt like there was no place for misfits like us. We all held our middle fingers high.

"Fuck you, Yankee Stadium," we said.

On the drive home after the court hearing, at which Butch was lectured by an incredulous ninety-year-old judge and charged with criminal mischief, we were tired and drifting silently into our own orbits, bracing for the indignities of the days and weeks to come. No one had said anything for a long time. I remember that the song on the radio was that insipid virus of a ditty, "Walking on the Sun," a clear sign that we had ceased giving a shit. You know, let whatever comes, come. My brother was at the wheel, driving the used car he'd bought with advance money for a travel book he would never complete. We crossed over the Macombs Dam Bridge, in the shadow, as they say, of Yankee Stadium.

"I remember you, scumbags," Yankee Stadium must have said, squinting down at us.

If memory serves, there's a somewhat unusually placed traffic light at the end of the Macombs Dam Bridge. Or maybe it isn't normally there and Yankee Stadium put it there just for that moment. Anyway, it changed from yellow to red. My brother's mind was elsewhere. A car barreled straight at us, eyes getting wide in the faces of all its passengers.

Brakes squealed, then came the sound of crunching metal.

You could certainly make the case that Yankee Stadium was merciful in its revenge. No one in either car was physically harmed in the head-on collision. But after my brother was able to nurse his convulsing vehicle to the shoulder, where the team of young muscular Bronx residents from the other car commenced screaming at him, I watched my brother age before my eyes. His posture sagged. His face went gray. He was barely getting by as it was. He had let his insurance payments lapse. He was getting screamed at and berated. His car, which he needed to complete the travel book he had been contracted to write, was clearly now no more than a few heartbeats away from flatlining. Butch and I looked on, Butch freshly saddled with the criminal mischief charge, me with the sad feeling that came from watching my older brother, who I'd always idolized, standing there in the middle of it all like a pitcher with nothing left and no help on the way. A mop-up man who has to just stay in the box and take a beating as the boos rain down.

So I didn't give Yankee Stadium the finger a couple weeks ago. But it seemed to me that I ought to try to go beyond mere superstitious restraint. The phrase "what goes around comes around" came to mind, so I tried to reach for a more positive farewell to the doomed ballpark than mere silence. But I couldn't come up with anything in that moment. I thought first about all the painful games I'd been to there. I thought about the subway ride home from one of those games, when my brother and I glared wordlessly at a guy in a Yankee cap who laughed richly and deeply, a millionaire's laugh, his tan arms around two beautiful women, a moment that seemed to sum up for us our placement in that city of have-nots and haves. I thought of all the bad moments that I'd watched on TV, too, everything all the way up to Aaron Boone. Then of course I also took a swallow of that inexhaustible elixir that is Game 7 of the 2004 American League Championship Series, the moment that, coupled with the subsequent sweep in the World Series of the Cardinals, made everything OK. But I decided not to mention this moment to Yankee Stadium. I didn't want to get in a head-on collision.

In the end I said nothing, just drove, my middle fingers tucked in next to all my other fingers, both hands firmly on the wheel at ten and two.

But as the day went on I continued thinking about Yankee Stadium, as if something was prodding me to push beyond the cycle of spite and suffering and revenge.

II

I ended up thinking about the early 1990s. I ended up thinking about Phil Rizzuto, Steve Balboni, and Deion Sanders.

I'd moved to New York at that time, during what was, for me, a mercifully peaceful lull in the Yankees' decades of dominance, the team guttering at the ragged end of what for the Yankees had already been an interminable playoff drought.

I had moved to the city just after finishing college, with no idea what to do with my life. My brother was already living in the city, as was my dad, so I drifted there by default, in a style diametrically opposed to the myth—most purely distilled in the song belted by Sinatra after Yankee victories—of the bright-eyed New York, New York newcomer bent on conquest. Had the Yankees, the team that had while haunting my childhood contributed to my general existential belief that I couldn't win, been their usual bullying selves upon my meek, cringing arrival in New York, I might have curled up into a fetal position forever.

Lucky for me, they were putrid, laughable, their games on television often spooling quickly into insignificance, where the warm, welcoming light of the star named Phil Rizzuto always shone brightest. With the Scooter presiding, Yankee games became for me a way to enjoyably pass the time. It was the same when I went to the Stadium, unless I was foolish enough to go to a game when the Red Sox were in town, when all old wounds were reopened. If they were playing anyone but my team, I could spread myself out across a couple seats in the sparsely populated upper deck and bask in the sun and sip a beer and live for a while in a world utterly free of consequence.

It was just what I needed at that difficult time, an escape from time, from the feeling that I was hurtling forward into a life I wasn't ready for and would surely bungle. For however much time it took for the Yankees to squander another chance at victory, I was neither here nor there. I was just watching base-ball and nothing mattered.

I usually shared these afternoon sanctuaries with my brother, who was struggling just as much as I was with this new lemon of a vehicle called adulthood. Gradually, our focus came to center on one of the players on the Yankees' sprawling roster or retreads and misfits, their balding mustachioed top-heavy slugger, Steve Balboni.

Balboni enacted his last comically simple all-or-nothing at-bats for the Yankees during those years. We loved him. In a complicated world he made everything simple: he would either strike out or blast a home run, nothing else. More than that, he seemed sincere. I don't think the term sincerity gets used much in the evaluation of an athlete's performance, but there was something about Balboni that communicated this trait. We sent him a letter, told him how we admired him. A few weeks later, we got a letter back, a nice note from his wife. A sincere exchange, one of the few in our halting, irony-choked lives.

In years to come I would come to think that I had witnessed Steve Balboni hit a game-winning home run at Yankee Stadium, which would have marked the lone time in my life where I would have stood up and cheered for a Yankee. I understand now that this memory is faulty, and that it was my brother who was at that game and told me about it.

When I realized this I thought that I was left without a happy Yankee-related memory from Yankee Stadium. The best I could do by way of farewell was simply not hold up a middle finger.

Then I recalled one early 1990s summer day when I sat in the upper deck with a friend, the two of us spread across several seats, taking our leisure. I don't remember who was winning. A fly ball was lofted to left field. The Yankees' young left fielder, Deion Sanders, circled under it, looking a little unsure, like someone who had just had a bright light blasted in his eyes.

Dear Yankee Stadium: The ball hit him in the head and fell to the grass. Dear Yankee Stadium: I was laughing. I was happy. I was glad to be alive.

CHARLES PIERCE

It was a bright Sunday morning, a soft August day in Yankee Stadium in the Bronx in New York City. The blue of the sky and the green of the field and the fragile white of the latticework façade in the upper decks all seemed to snap in the clear air. I walked to the front of the press box and leaned over. I could hear the players going through batting practice, all muscular young profanity. There was a soft breeze on my face, and somebody behind me asked if I wanted ice cream. I leaned into the breeze. The last notes of the national anthem faded into rippling applause. Yes, I told my friend. I will have ice cream.

Why are we doing this, my son Abraham thought, as the car rolled west down Route 9 toward Shrewsbury. He would have spoken, but he didn't know what to say or how to say it. If he got angry about going, his mother might have understood, but Chas wouldn't. He might even think that Abraham hated the old man, and he didn't. His mother and Chas were in different realities, and Abraham felt he couldn't pray in one of them without cursing in the other. So he sat in the backseat of the car. It occurred to him that the memories were all beginning to blur.

Not just the memories of the house in Shrewsbury, but the rides themselves, blending together, becoming in his mind one long ride out and one long ride back. Himself, dozing off, over and over again, never quite sleeping and never fully awake. His mother, growing more tense by the mile. And Chas . . . well, Chas wasn't a part of this. When all the rides and all the Sundays blended into a single memory, Chas wasn't there. He was out of town. He was at a ball game. This Sunday had begun like all the rest of them.

Once they were at the house in Shrewsbury, Abraham dug in his heels. His mother was going to take his baby brother and Grandpa to a garage sale that people were having a little ways up the hill. He insisted that he come along. Grandpa was obviously displeased. At the yard sale, his mother bought Abraham some children's magazines and they all walked back down the hill to the house again.

Grandpa sat down on the couch again. Something on the television set caught Abraham's interest, and he settled in to watch it on the arm of the couch, at the end where Grandpa was sitting. His face blank, and without saying a word, my father leaned over and rammed Abraham with his shoulder. Abraham had the odd sensation of being briefly airborne before he tumbled to the floor. Grandpa Pierce was silent. Abraham didn't cry. He picked himself up, walked across the room, and sat in a chair. He watched as the storm broke around him.

Margaret saw what had happened. Horrified, she confronted my mother.

"Who asked you to do anything anyway?" my mother said. "We can get along without you. Go. Leave. Who cares?"

"We're not coming back," Margaret replied.

"Fine," said my mother. Margaret told Abraham to take his little brother out to the car.

Once she came out, Margaret kept repeating, "I am never coming back here again."

It sounded good to Abraham. It would be nice not to hate Sundays any more.

It was a dead-level time in the ball game. The shadows were longer, stretching and angling themselves out to the most distant parts of the outfield. I remember being caught up in an earnest debate with a friend of mine concerning the relative merits of *Duck Soup* vs. *Animal House*. We were so deeply engaged that I didn't hear my name at first.

"Charlie Pierce," the press box PA honked. "Phone call."

I left the debate there and walked past the long rows of seats toward the phone on the wall at the back of the press box. There was an old man in a blue jacket standing there. He handed me the phone. He walked slowly away.

Margaret wasn't yelling. Her voice shook but it was not loud. The words were a torrent, but they were not a cascade. She had stopped at a phone booth along Route 9. I could hear the trucks rushing past her as she spoke. She wanted me to come home that minute. Unless I did something about my father, something about my mother, something about something, Margaret was going to leave. She was going to take the kids and go to her parents' house. She'd had enough. I had no instincts to guide me. I talked just to talk. We agreed, finally, that I would stay for the rest of the game, because there wasn't any real difference between leaving for the airport at that moment, and leaving for the airport in an hour. I felt lost in my own life—not for the first time and, I suspected, not for the last. I'd been raised on time and distance.

It was how we functioned as a family, with uncles we rarely saw developing diseases we never talked about. Now there was no time, and there was less distance. I stayed there by the phone for the rest of the game. I could see only a sliver of the bright day. I could hear only the faintest echoes of the loudest cheers.

*Editor's note: This piece was originally published in the book *Hard to Forget: An Alzheimer's Story* (Random House, 2000) and appears here with the permission of the author.

KEVIN BAKER

There are so many to choose from, it's hard to pick just one. There's my first (and only) game in what was truly the old (pre-1976) Stadium, the first major league game I ever attended, back in 1967. It was against the California Angels, and as I recall Horace Clarke hit a home run, and Joe Pepitone lost the game on an error. Par for the course for the Yankees of that year.

There were the World Series clinchers in both 1996 and 1999. The 1996 game was especially thrilling, a very close contest with the crowd roaring continuously, and the stands literally shaking. It also featured tens of thousands of Yankees fans, waiting to get in, breaking into a "Fuck the Bra-a-a-ves!" version of their tomahawk chant.

Afterwards, people were carrying around a coffin, marked Atlanta Braves, like something from four or five decades ago. The 1999 clincher was a little less exciting—the Yanks already had a 3–0 lead in games, and Clemens shut the Braves down for most of the game—but it does stand out for watching Mariano Rivera break Ryan Klesko's bat three times in the ninth, reducing a team that was about to be swept in the World Series to helpless laughter.

I was also fortunate enough to be at Mo's playoff debut, in that fifteen-inning epic against Seattle, back in 1995. Here was this skinny little guy, coming out of the bullpen in extra innings, when we had nobody left, and throwing pure heat. It was a marvelous, crazy game, with Leyritz hitting that walk-off home run in the rain, and the Stadium misbehaving wildly.

So many games. . . . I was at David Wells's perfect game, thanks to my brother-in-law, the Twins fan. I remember rushing over from Shea in 1985, when both New York teams were fighting for first down the stretch. The Mets had won a thriller that afternoon against the Cardinals, and the Yanks beat the Blue Jays that night. The crowd was fired up, sensing a Subway Series, and when some poor woman who was singing the Canadian national anthem forgot the words they showered her with boos, almost starting an international incident.

So many memories . . . moments that remain for no particular reason, just the sheer beauty of the game. Like watching Pedro Martinez making his way out to the bullpen while storm clouds blackened and swelled before an evening game late in 2003. Or watching a windstorm sweep all the accumulated debris of the Stadium around and around the park, while waiting for the second game of a doubleheader to start one night back in 1980. Watching Sparky Lyle use the whole ballpark when he had nothing, making hitter after hitter crush towering, useless flyballs to Death Valley in the Stadium's old, original configuration. Or a broiling July day back in 1999, when there was (typically) no ice in the park, but no one cared too much because the Yanks were pounding Cleveland to sweep a three-game set.

There were the unexpected games, the delightful games. Like Opening Day 1978, when they handed out "Reggie!" bars to every customer, and Reggie Jackson responded by hitting a three-run homer in the first. One-by-one, then in flurries, then in a steady rain the small, square, orange-wrapped candy bars came floating down from the stands as Reggie toured the bases, like a tribute to some Spanish bullfighter.

On July 2, 1978, I saw Mickey Rivers bring his strange magic to the Stadium once again. Rivers was always a favorite of mine, an improbable star, a trickster icon. He was a weak-armed, erratic center fielder and a leadoff man who never liked to take a pitch, but somehow he had a way of doing the little thing that could break open the game. He came up to pinch-hit in about the seventh inning or so of this game, with the Yanks trailing Detroit 2–1 and one man on base, and immediately hit a long flyball to right-field. Mickey Stanley leapt to get it at the wall. About a dozen Yankee fans out in right field leaped for it, too. The ball bounded away.

Stanley, a veteran of fourteen major-league seasons, ran over to complain to the umpire that he had been interfered with. While he did, both Rivers and the runner in front of him went all the way around to score. The Yanks won, 3–2, in a year when they didn't have a game to spare. That same October, Rivers noticed that Bucky Dent's bat was cracked in the playoff game in Boston, and handed him another one . . .

So many moments. Every time Mariano Rivera came loping out of that bullpen. Every time Don Mattingly stood up there with that bulldog stance. Rickey Henderson reaching base, Dave Winfield vaulting up into the seats to take away a home run, the roll-call from the right-field bleachers every game . . .

My very favorite memory, though, had to be an epic game between the Yankees and Red Sox on July 1, 2004. This was, more or less, the last moment the Yanks still had the upper hand in the rivalry, and they were going for a three-game sweep at the Stadium.

It was a wonderful game, a game where all sorts of things happened, the lead changing hands again and again. It was a game that seemed as if it might never end, going on into extra innings, with each team threatening repeatedly, being stymied only by one outstanding play after another. Alex Rodriguez snagged a hot shot at third, stepped on the bag for the force, then made a great throw from his knees to the plate to get the Yanks out of a bases-loaded, no-out situation. A little later, Derek Jeter made his now famous run and grab of a sinking, Trot Nixon pop-up with the bases loaded again, plunging headlong into the left-field stands and cutting his face open.

There were more theatrics, right up to the end. Manny crushed a titanic home run in the top of the thirteenth, only to see the Yanks come back yet again, with two outs and nobody on in the bottom of the inning, on three, booming hits from Miguel Cairo, Ruben Sierra, and John Flaherty, of all people. It was a delirious, wonderful, startling game, with all the tension and the drama you could want.

But I think the image that stands out most for me was all the defensive shifts the Red Sox made when the Yankees loaded the bases a couple times themselves in extra innings, always with equal futility. Terry Francona put them into one desperate shift after another, bringing outfielders into the infield, and then back, so that in the late Bronx night the players were tossing their gloves back and forth to each other, a shower of leather flying through the air, making this epic, major league showdown seem for a moment like nothing so much as a boys' pick-up game.

That's my Yankee Stadium memory. I'll miss the dirty old thing.

MARK LAMSTER

In the summer after my junior year at college I got a job working in the records department of HIP, the health insurance agency. In a basement office with no windows, I'd review double-entry ledgers for typographical errors, a tedious process I considered beneath my dignity. It was depressing work, my colleagues were unfriendly, and the most humiliating part of it was that I was just short of incompetent. I didn't care, and it showed. Then I came home to a message from the New York Yankees. I was going to The Show.

As a budding sports journalist, I'd written to *Yankees Magazine*, offering my services as an intern. A spot had opened, and the next week I reported for duty at the Stadium, over-eager in khakis and a blazer. The office was in the dingy stadium basement: frayed carpet, no windows. My primary task was to proofread box scores and stat tables for the team's minor league affiliates—these went in the back of the magazine. Not much of an improvement from HIP, and the climate was no better. The secretary spent her days endlessly defending the integrity of Milli Vanilli, recently revealed to be a fraud, while playing their hit record on a boom box.

This was 1990, and things were bleak for the Yanks. Bucky Dent had been cashiered in favor of Stump Merrill, but the team was still heading for ninety-five losses and a seventh-place finish. The magazine's basement office, out of sight and out of mind, was actually a blessing. No one wanted to be upstairs, on the executive level. The Boss's comings were unpredictable, and the staff lived in a perpetual state of fear for his arrival. It was said that he'd fire employees on a whim, and for no reason other than appearing in his sightline. The place was terrorized—joyless, somber, tense. I'd never experienced anything like it. In my entire time working there, I met one player, Luis Polonia, which tells you everything you need to know about those Yankees. The highlight of my tenure was an elevator ride with Bobby Murcer. He wore white pants and a green plaid jacket—a joyfully loud ensemble—and made it a priority to greet every employee with his Oklahoma drawl. He was The Anti-Boss.

There was actually one perk to the job. It came with a Yankee ID, and with that I had free entry to as many games as I could stand. I could sit just about anywhere as well; the good seats were rarely occupied, and with a flash of the badge I was clear to do as I pleased. I rarely sat in those good seats. I preferred the bleachers out in right field, where I'd been a regular for years, along with my closest high school friends.

The play on the field was grim, but the bleachers were always a party, and the reason was Melle Mel, the founding genius behind Grandmaster Flash and the Furious Five. These were the days before "Roll Call," before the "Bleacher Creatures" became a self-professed institution. Mel was the unquestioned leader of the gang, and was usually accompanied by Busy Bee, a lesser light of the hip-hop stage.

The two knew how to get a crowd working; the bleachers were just another club. They usually arrived in about the third inning, rarely sober, often stoned. (I don't think I'm telling tales out of school here.) I remember them flying especially high one evening, and then returning home after the game to catch the last few minutes of Johnny Carson. On comes a PSA featuring Mel, "Don't Do It."

Mel's signature was a dead-on impersonation of Stevie Wonder doing "I Just Called to Say I Love You," which he'd sing waving his head to and fro while standing in the ass-contoured blue plastic seats that were removed about a decade ago, in favor of benches. (More fannies, more dollars.) Mel wore a ring with his name on it that stretched across his entire hand; it was a real danger during high fives. Whenever games got close in the late innings—this was known as "Toenail Time" for some inexplicable reason—he'd demand the entire bleachers stop drinking and pay full attention.

Mel gave the bleachers a bit of celebrity cache, but what really made his presence special was the sense he gave us that we were all—ghetto rappers, lunchpail types, old timers, Hispanics, even us privileged kids from Manhattan—a part of something uniquely New York, united in our devotion to the Yankees. He was a "star," and had a magnetic charisma, but he was inclusive. One night Busy came in with copies of his new album, passed them out to the crowd, and invited everyone to his set that night at the Palladium. I wish we had gone, though I suspect we would never have made it past the velvet rope.

I spent years of my life out in those bleachers. My friends and I developed our own traditions. After the game we'd take the 4 train back to Eighty-Sixth Street and, after a win, go for "victory donuts" at the shop on the corner of Lex. It wasn't always so fun. In 1988, after Steinbrenner had picked a fight with Don Mattingly over his haircut, I found myself on the back page of *Newsday*, sitting below a group of regulars holding up letters that spelled "TRADE GEORGE." We despised him, and though I'm no longer the despising kind, I can't say I've forgotten or forgiven his many trespasses and disgraces. Eventually, of course, Steinbrenner did himself in, and for conspiring against Dave Winfield, always Mel's favorite. And that was a new dawn for the Stadium, and the team.

By the mid-nineties, my friends and I stopped visiting the bleachers with regularity. Schedules intruded, girlfriends, lives. When we did go to the ballpark, and we still went often, we opted for better seats. The bleachers changed. The "Creatures" had begun to consider themselves an attraction, justifiably. With that new fame came unpleasant questions about authenticity, who was a true regular. Mel stopped showing up.

We were still fans, still true, and we got our ultimate reward in 1996. My greatest memory of Yankee Stadium comes from that year, and it wasn't even at the Stadium. I watched the last game of the World Series that year with my future wife in her tiny studio apartment on Eighty-Seventh Street and First Avenue. The joy of that game's final moment, Charlie Hayes clutching that last pop—the ultimate exaltation.

I had planned with my friends that, in the case of a win, we'd all meet up for one last victory donut. But somehow we found out that the Yanks would be holding their victory party that night at Cronies, a sports bar on Eighty-Seventh and Third, just a couple of avenues away. By the time we all met there the entire block was shut down and barricaded, fans were cheering and passing around champagne, and the players were arriving by limo—Derek, Tino, Jim Leyritz in a ten-gallon hat. For years, we had been trekking out to the Bronx to cheer on our team. Now, after the win we had all longed for, they came home to us.

GLENN STOUT

I t was a nothing game.

September 24, 1992. A Thursday night. The Yankees in fourth place and the Tigers in sixth, neither of them close to the Blue Jays, or, apparently, with any chance of ever getting close to the Blue Jays or anyone else atop the division for at least a few more years. A young Scott Kamienicki vs. an aging Frank Tanana, one-time hard thrower whose fastball had come and gone and left behind a pile of guts and guile.

We were down from Boston, my girlfriend and I. She'd recently moved back in with me after getting a grad degree from Columbia and living and working in Mount Vernon for a few years, and we had some business to take care of in the city.

It had already been a funny day. Taking a bus somewhere downtown I'd seen Liza Minelli poking around outside some antique bathroom fixture store. Down by City Hall I'd used one of those high-tech public bathrooms that had cost fifty cents and gave itself a shower afterwards, like something from *The Jetsons*. Then I saw Rudy Giuliani walking down the street.

We went to the game—a nice early fall night. Only about 12,000 people were in the Stadium, so we had pretty good seats, probably the best seats I'd ever had for a major league game anywhere at that point—the main boxes, not too high up, almost dead on a line with the left-field foul line. We might have paid $12 a ticket, which also would have been the most I'd ever spent on a baseball ticket at the time.

I saw Nicolas Cage. He had better seats, right behind the plate, but still twenty or thirty rows up.

There wasn't a whole lot of care on display on the field that night. Mattingly played hard, as always, and cracked a couple of doubles, and this new kid in center field, Bernie Williams, had a good night. But almost everyone else on either team—Charlie Hayes, Rob Deer, Tartabull—was packing it in; you could tell.

Seventh inning. Yankees ahead 4–0. Tanana throwing changeups off changeups and the occasional big sloppy curve—nothing much over eighty miles an hour. The crowd was already starting to file out.

Leading off, Gerald Williams. Rookie. I remember liking Gerald more than Bernie at first. He moved like a ballplayer, while Bernie moved like an antelope still wet from birth.

Gerald Williams hadn't done much so far—a fly out, a strikeout. But now Tanana, thirty-nine years old and in his nineteenth year of major league baseball, gave him a pitch.

Williams didn't miss it. I'll never forget the trajectory—almost straight down the line, a little hook to it like a golf shot, that one bright spot against the black going smaller . . .

And Gerald Williams watching it, and walking, slow toward first before, barely, breaking into a trot. His first major league home run.

I was watching him saunter toward first when I heard someone yelling, not just to get someone's attention, but REALLY yelling, I mean angry "I'm gonna ruin your face" kind of mad.

It was Frank Tanana. Pissed. Chewing Williams' ass out every step he took all around the bases for standing there and showing him up. And Williams did speed up—not much—just enough to let Tanana know he heard but at the same time not so much to let him think he had been intimidated. And Tanana kept yelling.

Baseball-Reference.com tells me that Pat Kelly followed with a walk and Bernie Williams, this time running like an adult antelope, tripled, knocking out Tanana, and the Yankees went on to win 10–1, but to be honest, I don't really remember much else about the game.

But I've got a great excuse. You see, when I was down by City Hall earlier that day, my girlfriend and I had applied for a wedding license. We went back the next day and got married in a ceremony that took precisely twenty-seven seconds.

Or about as long as it took Gerald Williams to run around the bases.

EMMA SPAN

God knows why, but out of all the dozens of games I've been to, the very first thing I think of when I hear the words "Yankee Stadium" is Game 6 of the 2004 ALCS. Why couldn't I flash back to some nice come-from-behind affair against the Sox, or one of those sharp Andy Pettitte Division Series wins over the Twins, or my first game with my dad as a kid, learning to keep score? No, I have to go back to a frigid and drizzly night, in the far reaches of the upper deck, sitting by myself because by the time I'd managed to log onto Ticketmaster, they only had single tickets left.

And somehow, it's actually kind of a nice memory. I was wearing just about every item of clothing I owned in a futile attempt to layer for warmth, topped off with my ancient and oversized Paul O'Neill T-shirt, and using a garbage bag I'd brought from home as a poncho. This was my first championship series game ever, so I was absolutely determined to enjoy myself, no matter what—alone, freezing, damp, broke, watching the Yankees engage in one of the greatest chokes in sports history against that loudmouth Schilling . . . I wasn't about to let anything get me down. (Plus, I was so *sure* they were going to pull it out the next night.)

There was an earnest, attractive young Japanese tourist couple on my left, wearing full-on plush Godzilla-head hats. They didn't speak much English, but the man did turn to me a few innings in and manage to ask why the crowd was booing Schilling for throwing over to hold the runner on first. "That's his job, yes?" he wanted to know, reasonably enough. While I was trying to figure out the best way to phrase my reply, the man to my right, who turned out to be named Joey, leaned over and beat me to it.

"Because Schilling's a fucking pussy!" he explained, cheerfully.

Joey, a thick guy in his forties in the classic old-school Brooklyn mold, was at the game with his buddy, who was also named Joey. They'd shared season tickets for just about forever, they said. The Joeys ended up buying me a couple beers, and we made friendly small talk in between Schilling's oozing bloody sock (which we couldn't see), the reversed home run call (which we also couldn't see, so we assumed the Yankees were robbed), and A-Rod's infamous slap play (which we *also* couldn't see, and so, of course, we were certain the umps had spectacularly blown the call).

There are different kinds of hecklers at the Stadium; some guys are mainly trying to be funny, some get genuinely, alarmingly furious and need to vent their rage. The Joeys were another type, the kind who see heckling as a job—part of their responsibility as fans, done seriously, with spirit but without bile. The Joey directly to my right alternated steadily between polite conversation and earsplitting obscene abuse directed towards the field.

Joey: FUCK YOU, DAMON, YOU SUCK!
YOU BALL-LICKING ASSHOLE! GET A FUCKIN'
HAIRCUT! . . . So, where do you live?

Me: Brooklyn, you?

Joey: Hey, yeah? Me too. What part?

Me: Park—

Joey: HEY UMP, WHY DON'T YOU KISS MY ASS,
YOU MOTHERFUCKING PIECE OF SHIT! YOU
HEAR ME ASSHOLE? . . . Sorry, what was that?

Me: Park Slope.

Joey: No kidding, I got an aunt in Park Slope. Hey, are
you done with that cup?

Me: Yeah . . .

Joey: [Hurls empty cup onto field] GO FUCK YOUR-
SELF, YOU BLIND SHIT-EATING BASTARD! YOUR
MOTHER'S A WHORE! . . . Thanks.

It was around this time that the riot police rushed out to
ring the field, which seemed like overkill to me; in the old
days you had to pretty much mobilize a mob and try to tear
players limb from limb on the base paths before security got
involved, was my understanding, but those days were long
gone by 2004. In any case, things eventually settled down,
the Yankees lost ignominiously, and it took me fifty full
minutes just to get to the subway, the crowds were so thick.
All the way out people chanted "NINE-teen EIGHT-teen!," the
last time I'd ever hear that at the Stadium. When I finally
got home, very late, I watched the highlights, heard all about
Schilling's sock, and was fairly shocked to discover that the
umps had been completely right on both controversial calls.
(Sorry, Randy Marsh! I made some very personal remarks in
the heat of the moment which, in retrospect, were probably a
bit uncalled for.)

I don't really know why that game sticks out to me so much;
I've been to the Stadium so many times over the years, and

often at better games, in better weather, with good friends and no riot police. But there it is. Probably the Yankees will never use this treasured memory of mine in any of their brochures for season tickets at the new Stadium, but that's okay—because as Aristotle once wrote, "memory is the scribe of the soul." Or, as Joey might have put it: "Those bastards can stick their fucking martini bar right up their fucking asses."

TONY KORNHEISER

The truth is: I hated the Yankees.
I am old enough to remember when there were three teams in New York, and I hated two of them. I was a Giants fan, and the blood oath of a Giants fan was to hate the Dodgers, and because whenever the Giants beat the Dodgers, and got into the World Series, they lost to the Yankees. I hated the Yankees, too.

I didn't give the Yankees much thought other than that.

I hated them. Case closed.

When Mantle and Mays were young and their talents were blossoming and scary, there was a debate over who was better. Not in my house. In my house we knew Mays was better. In my house the only reasonable response to this debate was to hate Mantle.

Because I hated the Yankees, I automatically hated Mantle. I hated DiMaggio. I hated Rizzuto. I hated Berra. I hated Ford. I hated them all. I understood how good they were—in a weaker league, I should point out—and I understood how much greater they were in a symbolic sense than the Giants, mostly because of the powerful iconic images of Babe Ruth and those damned pinstripes. I understood all that. It made me hate them even more.

Once I saw Billy Crystal on television, talking about how thrilled he was to go to Yankee Stadium for the first time; how amazed he was to walk into the Stadium, after driving with his father through the streets of the Bronx, where there was nothing but gray concrete for miles and miles, and then to see the green grass of the Yankee infield and outfield; how it thrilled him to his bones in a spiritual sort of way, even at nine years old. So I began to hate Billy Crystal for thinking that Yankee Stadium was the only stadium to have grass. Like the Giants didn't have grass? Are you kidding me? (And what was tough about this was that I actually knew Billy Crystal; we had played against each other in softball rec league games; I lived around the corner from his brother, Joel; I'd interviewed Billy, and written about him. He'd invited me to his shows. But the Yankee thing was as thick as time. So I crossed him off the list. What can I tell you?)

As a sportswriter I covered a lot of Yankee games. I was there the night Reggie hit three home runs off the Dodgers in the World Series. (That was bittersweet for me, because I hated both teams; I was hoping they'd be tied and play all night, and drop dead of exhaustion.) I was there for old timers' days, when DiMaggio would saunter through the clubhouse like a lord, and those crabby guys like Thurman Munson and Sparky Lyle would respectfully call him "Mister DiMaggio," and those guys didn't respect anybody. I was there for far too many of Billy Martin's mean-spirited tirades. I occasionally sat with George Steinbrenner, because I once wrote a long profile of him, and he threw me a bone here and there. I liked George, because he seemed to be the only one in the ballpark who understood that what it was really about to be a Yankee and a Yankee fan was social climbing. George understood the Gatsby lure of the whole joint.

What am I supposed to be writing about again? Yankee Stadium?

Yeah, a nice field.

Very small seats, some of them obstructed. Very steep ramps. Sort of shabby at the edges. Not what you'd call warm or friendly.

But nice in a WASPY sort of way.

You'd rather bring a date to Shea. But, okay, Yankee Stadium had its haughty charm.

It's funny because in that big Steinbrenner piece I tried to give the Yankees their due, and I wrote a few lines that went: "In the history of this country, there are, arguably, a number of myths that define who we are as a people. One is the frontier. One is the New England town meeting. One is New Orleans Jazz. Another is the New York Yankees." George liked that so much, he had large, royal blue banners made, with those very words in white, and he flew those banners in Yankee Stadium for years. For me, personally, he embossed the passage on a piece of glass, and sent it to me, framed over a swatch of those damned pinstripes.

I still hold it dear. And, of course, I loathe it.

In the old days, in the days before blogging and cell phones and facelifts, there was power in names. Not like today, when everything is sponsored, when companies fight to see how tall they can build their names on the outside of a ball field and plot to hijack a bowl game or a golf tournament.

In the old days, people didn't go to games to be seen there, and they didn't go all painted up like some nineteenth-century saloon whore. They went out of affection. Out of longing. Out of need. In the old days Yankee Stadium had a power nothing else in sports could match. In the old days Yankee Stadium stood for the power and the promise of America.

Now there's a new Yankee Stadium, huh?

So I guess the old days are gone.

THE NEW STADIUM: FIRST IMPRESSIONS

ALEX BELTH

When I got off the D train at 161st Street Yankee Stadium, the sun was still high in the sky, a perfect spring evening to see the new Yankee Stadium for the first time. But coming up from the subway, I stopped dead in my tracks. Here it was, game day—a preseason exhibition against the Chicago Cubs—and the old Stadium, the place that held so many memories for me that it was like a second home, was empty.

It seemed unfair, building the new, sparkly place right next to the old one, then I reminded myself, "Hey, at least it's better than schleppin' out to Jersey."

I remembered my last time at the old place, sitting in black seats at three in the morning after the Yankees played their final game there in September of '08, next to where Reggie Jackson's third home run landed in the '77 Series. I hung around until six working on a story about a longtime Yankee employee named Ray Negron. That day I followed Negron as he gave a two-hour tour of the place to a party of four headlined by Richard Gere, and stood on the field with Ray during the opening ceremonies, the packed house blinking with camera flashes. Later, when the place was close to empty, Ray and I took batting practice in the indoor hitting cage. Then I walked alone on the damp outfield grass, finally standing in the bald patch in right field, and marveled at how imposing those upper decks looked.

Now I looked at the old Stadium and remembered through the years, seeing a burn victim with a boom box on his lap listening to "Kashmir" while he smoked a joint; watching with my father and brother in the upper deck behind home plate when Bobby Murcer hit a game-winning home run in extra innings; stuffing my disappointment with junk food one day when Reggie wasn't in the line-up; being thrilled another night when I got to see him hit a dinger; watching a gang of suburban meatheads screaming "Farmingdale" and throwing coins at a homeless man outside of Gate 6; being startled at how the place shook in October when the Yankees scored a run. I also remembered the bathrooms. Man, I hated those goddamn bathrooms.

Picture me: ten years old, sixty-five pounds soaking wet. I'm at the game with my mom and younger brother. It's the third inning and already I need to pee. I'm geeked to be there, the Yanks, my hero Reggie, so I hold it. By the sixth inning, I'm about to burst. Can't cheer, can't clap. Hunched over, chewing on my nails. I just gotta pee. I finally tell my mom and she tells me where to go and I venture off on my own. I knew how to get on a bus by myself and I wanted to be grown so damn bad I should be man enough to find the men's room and pee.

I inch my way down the ridiculously steep upper deck stairs, holding fast to the railing, bladder cramping, ahead of me all the green of the ball field and the gold reflection of the court building. I reach the bathroom and it is filled with smoke and the sounds of unruly, drunk men. It smells of sweat, beer, and piss. I wait for a stall to open, walk in and am greeted by a mess of cigarette butts, toilet paper, and shit. The walls are narrow, the voices booming behind me, and I can't pee. I must, but I can't. Someone bangs on the stall and shouts and I hear laughing. Shiver, shrivel—bubkus. I go back to my seat in defeat (later, mom takes me back down where I will myself to relief).

The food and the service at the old Stadium were just as foul as the restrooms. I once went to get a pretzel in the third inning of a game to find out that the concession stand didn't have any warm ones yet. When I expressed my surprise, the girl behind the counter screwed up her face and looked at me like I asked her for a loan.

Still, I stared now at the old Stadium and didn't want to leave it, warts and all. A few other fans stopped briefly too—"Hey, quick get my picture with the old Stadium"—but most of the gathering crowd was absorbed with the fresh sight in front of them: the new Yankee Stadium. The old place, still imposing, would be dismantled over a sixteen-month period of time, a Death Star in reverse.

I went through the turnstile and into the new building, unsure of what to feel or think. I wasn't offended by the new place as many of my friends were—you know, the Woody Allen "change equals death" crowd, or the ones burdened by a sense of moral conscience—but I wasn't jonesin' for a mallpark in the Bronx, either. Like most New Yorkers, I felt resigned to it.

I was immediately impressed by the spaciousness of the Great Hall. Sunlight poured into the room. I dug the banners and photographs of the great Yankee players strewn among the multitude of stores and food stands, vivid and brilliant. Up at the food court, there are photos of Babe Ruth holding a string of fish, Joe DiMaggio sipping a cup of tea, and Reggie Jackson eating a Reggie Bar in front of a poster of the Reggie Bar.

But the first view of the field, that dramatic moment which reminds us of being kids, has changed and not necessarily for the better. At the old place, the first glimpse of green was as viscerally exciting for me as when the lights go down in a movie theater. You climbed through a maze of concrete ramps and then up a narrow walkway before you saw grass, tension building every step of the way. It never got old, waiting in childlike anticipation for the renewed experience. At the new Stadium, once you approach the wide concourses on the field or the upper deck level, the first thing you notice is the space. There is nothing confined about it. Your eye is immediately greeted by light and openness, killing the suspense of that initial panorama. My first view of the field evoked no reaction—more like a non-reaction—and certainly no sense of wonder.

I walked around before I went to my seat because that's what everyone else seemed to be doing. Plus there was room to move, a dramatic change. The new Stadium is oriented towards an experience that is nomadic, not communal. Why stay in your seat when you can stroll the premises, have a drink at the Hard Rock Café or check out the Stadium store? There's even a window where you can stop and watch a high-end, Zagat-rated butcher at work. If you like what you see, you can order a $15 steak sandwich. The food is diverse and expensive—from dry sushi to Johnny Rockets—and not especially memorable (and if you are from the Rattle-Your-Jewelry set, there are exclusive, high-end restaurants, that were conspicuously empty on this night). At any given time, thousands of preoccupied fans are out of their seats roaming, and the concourses are deceptively tricky to navigate, with so many people walking and texting or talking into their cell phones. Many think nothing of getting up and shuffling past you in the middle of a pitch, not being rude, just clueless, doing what the ballpark invites them to do.

Another difference is the public address system. At the old Stadium, music and special effects projected out of three speakers in center field, accounting for the famous echo, echo. There is no echo anymore, and I missed it. Sure, it created hot spots, especially in sections of the upper deck, where the music was deafening, but it also created ambiance. Now, the soundtrack is evenly piped throughout the park via smaller speakers.

By consensus the whole place feels bigger than the old park even though there are fewer seats. It's not as steep but wider in the hips, and it seemed smaller to me, dwarfed by the mammoth HDTV at the centerpiece of the scoreboard section high above center field. The TV is so captivating, so impossibly clear, that it overshadows the field and serves to shorten the space between home plate and the outfield. The image on the screen dares you not to watch it; when a fifty-foot Derek Jeter appeared I had to resist the impulse to genuflect. But it is not only the TV that cuts to live action as a Yankee circles the bases after hitting a home run, it is all the other billboards, each one brighter than the next—Delta, Pepsi, Bank of America, Dunkin' Donuts . Those billboards generate a beam of light that forms a band around the stadium on the upper deck façade, a relentless Life Saver–like ring of advertisements. I left the place unable to blink. My eyes bulged out of my head like I was Marty Feldman.

But before I took off I paid a visit to the bathroom. Saved the best for last. The only reason I put it off is because I knew no matter how offended part of me would be by the new Yankee Stadium, I knew that's where the greatest improvement would be. And once I went there I'd be a convert no matter how much I missed the old joint.

Sure, it may not be as hard for me to take a leak in a public urinal as it was in the old days, but I will still duck into a stall without shame. So I was immediately comforted by the big clean-lit space of the bathroom. Lots of sinks, soap, towels, urinals, and stalls, evenly spaced and ample. You know, like they have in arenas in other cities like Los Angeles or San Antonio or Denver, just not in New York. At the risk of being mistaken for a dude who depends on Depends, I went into five different bathrooms all around the park and got a peaceful, easy feeling in all of them—the less than dulcet sounds of John Sterling and Suzyn Waldman piped into the speakers embedded in the walls, with the crowd noise muted behind it.

History has a NEW HOME, in case you hadn't heard. That's the slogan we've heard ad nauseam on TV and the radio all winter. Can't get the stupid loop out of my head. The swelling horns, the full monty Yankee reverence—extra fatty schmaltz. Fans gobbling up food and spending money on gear—T-shirts, jerseys, and hats—an orgy of consumer comfort. History's new home.

The Yankees' mallpark is going to take more than a little getting used to. Part of the old Stadium's charm was that it crammed a lot of people together with little attention to aesthetics or frills. The main point was clear: you were there to watch a game. Didn't matter if the food and the bathroom and the service ran from indifferent to indecent. Now, as in all of the newer parks, baseball is almost a sideshow. There is more to distract you so that there is a little less game and a little less of the special feeling that we got from the old Stadium. The palatial restrooms are more than welcome, but the purist in me regrets the change and I mourn the loss of another great city landmark that is now part of our past, vanishing New York.

NEIL DEMAUSE

For my first visit to the new Yankee Stadium, I prepared by whipping myself into a frenzy of anticipation and dread. This was, after all, the building I'd never wanted to see built, the monument to George Steinbrenner's hubris that was replacing my beloved House That Ruth Built, where I'd witnessed no-hitters, World Series games, and George Brett's infamous run-in with pine tar. But for better or for worse, it was also the Yankees' new home, and I wanted to see if they'd done a good job of doing a bad thing. The occasion was an open batting practice the day before the official exhibition opener, to which the Yankees had invited Bronx residents, as a bone to locals who'd been forced to put up with the demolition of their neighborhood park for the Yanks' new home. (New parks are supposed to open on the site of the old Stadium once it's demolished, but by then five parkless years will have passed.) I don't live in the Bronx, but I have friends who do, and through contacts at the local community board they'd landed me a coveted golden ticket to pre-opening day.

There were four of us: myself, two journalists for a Bronx community newspaper, and a neighborhood activist who'd helped lead the failed fight to stop the stadium. We waited in line at the new Gate 8, waved our tickets at the e-reader turnstiles, and ascended the new concrete steps, passing huge puddles of standing water from rain earlier that day. We emerged into the bleachers, a poured concrete beach with a panoramic view of the new stadium laid out before us.

We stopped. We stared. We struggled for words to describe the scene, at once familiar and unfamiliar. "It looks a lot like the old place." "Underwhelming." We watched as a Yankee employee swept a two-inch-deep puddle of water into a poorly placed drain.

Finally, my mind clicked. "Grand Theft Auto," I said. "It looks like a version of Yankee Stadium you'd see rendered in Grand Theft Auto. Only it'd be called something like Bomber Field, and everything would be subtly wrong."

Walking around the new Stadium only confirmed my sense of unease. The Yankees had made a huge deal about how the design was inspired by the original 1923 ballpark, but aside from the frieze (what generations of fans have erroneously called "the façade") ringing the upper deck, the new stadium felt less like that giant, shadowed barn than like the 1970s model redone in 2000s upscale-shopping-mall chic. Where the old stadium had felt oddly human-scaled for a 57,000-seat behemoth—I remember a visiting friend from Boston on her first trip looking up and saying in surprise, "Oh. This is ... nice"—the steeply cantilevered upper deck had been replaced by a layer cake of sub-levels reaching to the sky. And the most prominent feature, aside from the ad board ringing the entire grandstand, was the Moat, the sunken walkway separating the recliner-style seats of the high rollers paying $2,000 a pop in the front rows from the mere three-digit spenders in the seats behind them.

So much ink had been spilled about the "grandeur" of the new place, with its Hard Rock Café and sushi concession, that I half-expected to find staircases of polished marble and ushers wearing cummerbunds. Instead, everywhere was poured concrete and cheap-looking steel mesh and aluminum panels; navigating the confusing maze of ramps and stairways and blind exits, I would occasionally stumble past a sea of exposed exhaust manifolds servicing the concessions stands below. The only place it dazzled was in the concessions concourses themselves: Row upon row of food and souvenir stands (even, for some reason, a Peter Max art gallery), all designed so that you could watch the game while waiting for your pulled pork sandwich. Inside the seating bowl itself, though, the experience felt oddly generic: a bit like being at Yankee Stadium, a bit like Chicago's 1990s-era U.S. Cellular Field, a bit like Detroit's Comerica Park, and a bit like nowhere at all in particular. One bleacher regular arrived at his new seats and immediately exclaimed, "I feel like I'm on the road!"

I ascended to the top deck, knowing that if I were ever going to see a game here, this would be my vantage point. (Seats in the lower levels, which indeed have stunning views of the field, now start at $90 a pop.) I climbed to the last row, and confirmed my back-of-the-envelope estimates that though the new stadium has 7,000 seats fewer than the old, the combination of wider leg room for the moneyed classes down front and an upper deck set back to avoid casting the hoi polloi into shadow means that the cheap seats up top are a good bit farther from the action. Never again, I knew, would I see a scene like the one in the mid-eighties, when White Sox second baseman Julio Cruz casually played catch with a fan in the front row of the upper boxes—that upper deck, where you felt like you were suspended over the action, was an experience gone forever.

Eventually, I sat myself down in a seat in the front of the upper deck—at $70 still probably beyond my budget, but maybe someday I could sneak past the Yankees' newly reinforced army of security and watch the late innings of a game from there. Far below, Yankee players had emerged onto the field and were gathered around the batting cage in a ritual I'd watched hundreds of times before. The sun was out, delivering that warmth that makes baseball such an effective harbinger of the return of spring. If I tuned out the stadium itself, its ad strips and $12 buckets of "souvenir popcorn," I could almost forget that I was at the new place atop the ruins of Macombs Dam Park, instead of across the street at the old one. It was, after all, still baseball.

A roar rose up from the sprinkling of fans around me. My eyes darted to the field: Was something going on down by the batting cages? I looked around and finally found the source: the giant hi-def video screen perched above centerfield was showing Derek Jeter and Johnny Damon in the batting cage, joking and laughing in perfect clarity. The images on the screen were, if possible, clearer and more lifelike than the actual scene unfolding below. It was transfixing, and everyone around me was watching it, not the field itself.

I ran for the subway as fast as I could.

TYLER KEPNER

The new Yankee Stadium is different from the other new ballparks, and this is how it has to be. The Yankees, after all, are an institution and a state of mind like no other. They are not the Orioles or the Reds or the Rangers or the Mariners. They are the Yankees, and they embrace all that their brand connotes.

They are imperial and imposing, regal and righteous, stately and superior. And that is how the new Yankee Stadium feels. It is not intimate. It is grand, a palace more than a park. It conforms to the character of its tenant.

A carousel spins behind the third base seats in Detroit. A train chugs above the outfield in Houston. Fans in Phoenix frolic in a swimming pool. It works for them. It would not work in the Bronx. The Yankees have no names on their jerseys, no mascot romping through the stands, and no corporate sponsor splashed atop their marquee. That is their way.

To be sure, the new Yankee Stadium could have been more thoughtfully designed. The concrete walkway dividing most of the lower seating bowl disrupts the sense of community in the stands. The fences in the seating area are a charmless prison gray. Monument Park, which should have been the centerpiece, is buried beneath a hulking sports bar.

But the amenities are terrific, and the facilities for the players, the press, and the suite-holders are probably the best in the majors. Appropriately, the team's tradition is felt most acutely in the precise spot where it should be: at the entrance to the home clubhouse.

There, upon opening the double doors near the manager's office, you find a navy blue wall with a giant interlocking "NY," also in navy blue, in the middle. Surrounding it is a blizzard of silver signatures. Everybody who has ever played, managed, or coached for the Yankees can sign the wall. Nobody else.

Before Game 1 of the World Series, Wade Boggs inked his name within the logo. That is the most sacred spot of all. The only other names there are Yogi Berra, Whitey Ford, Reggie Jackson, Goose Gossage, and Dave Winfield. The Hall of Famers.

There is a similar display at the ballpark museum, signed baseballs from as many living Yankees as the team could find. But the authenticity of this one makes it special. It is intended for the people who call the clubhouse home, the ones charged with carrying on the tradition the stadium celebrates. It is by Yankees and for Yankees, a treasure of the House That George Built.

MARILYN JOHNSON

I'm standing in the breezy and spacious aisle in Yankee Stadium, looking down at the field where another great game is being played. The sweet air circulates; sun bathes the players. I rode a nice commuter train to get here; no woes or worries or $25 parking spots. The walk from the station to the park was pleasant. Now I'm free to stroll the boulevard of food and drink and baseball commerce, not crowded but still part of the crowd. The open architecture makes me happy.

When the announcement came that the old Stadium was doomed and a new one would be built next door, I was appalled. Why would the Yankees waste a perfectly good home, their shrine, and a ton of money to aggravate the good people of the neighborhood? The waste and expense and bullying politics still bother me. . . . and yet, forgive me: I feel as if I've been released from a prison. Consider the old Stadium without sentiment, if you can. It was a concrete bunker, a battle to get into it and a battle to leave. Remember the stony-faced guards who wouldn't let anyone pass during "God Bless America"? They proved it was possible to feel claustrophobic outdoors. Like all fans, I'd eat and drink and have no place to throw garbage except underfoot. That's right: By the end of the game, we were sitting in a dumpster. And it was a special hell for women: How many innings did I lose lining up for those foul restrooms? When the show was over and Frank crooned our exit song, we were squeezed out of the stadium into the hamster tube that led to the parking lots and the long stop-and-go ride home.

From this new, beautiful perch, with the game and the crowd arrayed before me, I find I don't miss a thing about the old park. Let the wrecking ball do what wrecking balls do. I'm home.

TED BERG

"Oh boy," I said in anticipation as a couple of Mariners fans wearing Jay Buhner jerseys filed in to the row of bleachers in front of us.

But nothing happened. Maybe one half-assed catcall from the trio behind us, a father and his two grown sons.

I looked around. What did I miss? Had no one noticed?

"That shit," I said to my fiance, "would never fly at the old place."

It started drizzling, and my lady was looking to buy her brother a T-shirt. The concourses, sheltered and luxuriously wide with all sorts of stores and museums and shiny things to stare at, beckoned.

As we walked, I felt alarmingly comfortable. In so many ways, the place looked familiar, like the old Yankee Stadium I respected. But it was sanitized, Disneyfied like Times Square.

The old place terrified me. I grew up a Mets fan, not hating the Bombers but not caring for them either. As a baseball fan first and foremost—one committed to seeing as many games as possible—I spent plenty of time in the Yankee Stadium bleachers.

Before games, I'd pore over my wardrobe, rifling through my closets to find something that could help me blend into the crowd without making me feel like a sellout. I never wanted to stand out, but I never wanted to entirely fit in, either.

And when I got there, when I sat in the bleachers and watched the games, I did so in trembling horror that someone or something I did might out me as a Mets fan. I knew what happened in the Yankee Stadium bleachers when something like that became public; the heckling and the harassment and the section-wide chants of "asshole."

They were animals in the old place, lapping up booze, squealing, feeding, barking. Chaotic and frenzied beasts, waiting to pounce on and devour the first jackass with the wrong hat or who picked the wrong time to cheer.

So now, dodging tweens with shopping bags and negotiating the mob crowded around the guy slicing up $16 steak sandwiches, I wondered if some important part of the Yankee legacy—something woven from the very fabric of New York—had been rubbed out or paved over or in some other way, destroyed with the closing of the old Stadium.

Steaming trays of chicken parmigiana caught my eye, so we got on line for sandwiches, and I reminisced about the old Stadium while awaiting the trappings of the new one. When we reached the counter, I pointed to the food.

"Two chicken parm heroes, please."

The guy nodded at the trays, acknowledging them, then reached into a drawer below his cash register and pulled out two pre-made, pre-wrapped sandwiches.

The old bait-and-switch. My fiance gasped. She started to protest, but I stopped her with a look. It was the old fear returning. Remember, honey: we're Mets fans. Don't draw attention to yourself in the belly of the beast.

With the rain abating, we returned to the bleachers, sandwiches in hand. The wholesome family sitting behind us had apparently spent the entirety of our absence slamming back beers. The two sons were now antagonizing the Seattle faithful sitting in front of us, one of whom finally turned around.

"Shut up, you fat piece of shit!"

The father calmly leaned toward his son.

"Kick his fucking ass, Tommy!"

And he did. Or he tried. To be honest, I was too busy shielding the woman I love to recount the blow-by-blow, but punches were thrown and punches were landed, and I realized how wrong I was to fear that I no longer had anything to fear. The bleachers in Yankee Stadium were as terrifying as ever.

You could build an $8 billion replica of Shangri-La out of marshmallow fluff, but fill it up with denizens of the Yankee Stadium bleachers, and it'll still scare me yellow. The new park might look like a shimmering, disinfected shopping-mall version of the old place, with the big fancy scoreboards and fine-dining options and the Hard Rock Café, but it's still filled up with precisely the same assholes.

The old bait-and-switch.

Cops descended quickly to escort the Mariners fans out of the building that night. The aggressors were spared the same fate when they produced badges of their own. They were off-duty but charged instead with defending an entirely different sort of justice.

And with the law enforced, they returned to their beer.

Derek Jeter had a big hit to put the Yanks ahead in the eighth. Mariano Rivera locked down the save with a 1–2–3 ninth. I sat through it all furtively, my nerves somehow quieted by the familiar dread.

MARSHA DREW

Todd was never accused of doing anything halfway. He thought every American should know and love baseball; he thought it was sad if you did not know about the game and its history. Todd grew up outside of Syracuse, the former home of the Yankees Triple-A team, which is how he became a Yankees' fan. When we moved there early in our marriage, he took me to minor league ballparks all around upstate New York and taught me the game.

Todd even had me going to Hall of Fame inductions in the heat of the summer and SABR (Society for American Baseball Research) meetings over the winter. Years ago, we were at a SABR meeting in Cooperstown—only baseball diehards go to Cooperstown in the winter—and after the meeting, one of the wives of a SABR founding member stood up, an adorable older woman, started clapping, and said, "Good show boys, good show." That stuck with Todd. After Yankee wins, when the guys walk out on the field and shake each other's hands, Todd would always clap until the last player was off the field and would say, "Good show boys, good show."

We moved to New York in June of 2002 and had full-season tickets from 2003 on. Todd was religious about scoring the game. He really concentrated. We'd often sit there and not say a word for several innings. I'm grateful that we shared those times at the ballpark together as a couple. It is something that will stay with me for the rest of my life. I will always be able to go to a baseball game and enjoy it. Now, I miss the small things—breakfast before the game at the Crown Diner on 161st street on a Saturday, or grabbing a doughnut on the way home, or sitting in Joyce Kilmer Park between split double headers, all those little things, the shared moments.

Because we had full season tickets it put us in a good position for the first year in the new Stadium. The new seats were dead-on, the same distance and angle as our old seats. The grass is cut the same, the mound is the same color—I can actually forget that I am at the new Stadium sometimes. Todd would think the new park is over the top, that it caters to the people in the corporate boxes, and is altogether more than a baseball fan needs to watch a game, but I think he would have liked the actual field.

Todd is with me in spirit when I am at the new Stadium. I catch myself turning and saying, "So how many strikeouts does this pitcher have?" When I am at the Stadium, I always sit in Todd's seat, not my own. If I sat in my old seat, it would be hard having someone besides Todd sitting next to me in his seat. That's still too much to bear. I bought our seats from the old Stadium and have them out on my little balcony, and I feel especially close to Todd when I sit in his seat.

I went to about fifteen games during the regular season in 2009 and the three World Series games. I sold a handful of the regular season tickets on Stub Hub, but mostly I distributed them to our friends, family, and colleagues as a way to say thank you to all of the people who have been so supportive and helpful since Todd died.

A few months after Todd passed away I moved back down to North Carolina, where I grew up, to be closer to my family. But I flew up for the three World Series games in New York. I had to be there. I knew that it would be emotional, but I would have never forgiven myself had I not gone. I took my father to the first two games—he had never been to a World Series game, and it was special to have him there. My dad did not know Todd well, but he was there with me during Todd's surgery and stayed well over a week afterwards to support me—he even handled organizing Todd's memorial service. Dad was like a five-year-old when I asked him to come with me to the Series, a special thrill for me because I never know what to get him for a gift. The first night was very cold, windy, and rainy. Cliff Lee pitched a great game for the Phillies, but Dad had a blast, and we both enjoyed the second night much better.

For the final game, I took Gabriel, the twelve-year-old son of Todd's best friend, Michael. Gabriel is an impressive baseball player himself, and he and Todd got along extremely well. I've been to numerous games with Gabriel over the years, and I do not think he has ever gotten out of his seat during the game, a trait he shared with Todd. At Game 6, I was afraid I was going to bawl my eyes out, so I told Gabriel if I got upset not to worry, that I would be okay.

As the innings ticked away and the twenty-seventh World Series Championship was getting close, I was amazed that I was not nervous. When I watched a game with Todd, he would get so uptight that I would be nervous too. In between at-bats or pitches, he'd tuck his scorebook under his arm and put his pencil behind his ear and clap. He clapped until his palms were red. And he would have such a serious look on his face. "Todd," I'd say, "are you breathing? Remember to breathe." At some point during Game 6, I turned to Gabriel and said, "You

218 ·   Lasting Yankee Stadium Memories

know, it is weird, I'm not nervous because Todd is not sitting here."

When the Yankees won the Series and were celebrating on the field, I stood there with tears running down my cheeks. Todd would have been so proud of them, and thrilled for Alex Rodriguez. I was emotionally spent, but I still clapped as hard as I could, cheered until I was hoarse, and listened to Todd, "Good show boys, good show."

AFTERWORD:
ADDITIONAL MEMORY

The old women sat in the back of the room next to the kitchen with their hands folded in their laps. There were four of them. They whispered to each other and looked after the children as the men sat on the black leather couch and suede chairs in the front of the room watching the World Series on TV.

I was there with my friend Jesse who I'd come to know through Bronx Banter. This was the apartment of one of his high school pals. His old crew attended JFK High School in the Bronx and was still close. I'd gotten to know them during the Yankees' playoff run in 2009. The Yanks kept winning games—dramatic, improbable victories—and since you don't mess with a good thing I kept watching with them.

One runs a nightclub with his uncle on Dyckman, another owns a batting cage in Kingsbridge, but most of them are cops. It was at the hitting cage that we'd watched most of the post-season, but now we were in the more formal apartment setting for Game Six of the Series.

I sat on the edge of a chair next to the couch, my cell phone resting on my right knee. The Yankees scored early and built a good lead, and each time the Yanks plated a run the men slapped five hard and yelled. It was a fine time, but I missed my wife, Emily. She was at home watching the game, and though we kept in constant touch, texting each other as the innings passed, it wasn't the same as being together.

The Yankees were ahead by plenty, so there wasn't much tension for the last few innings. Jesse was going to drop me off at home after the game. I was happy to be with these dudes but wanted to see the last out of the season with the woman who never expected to become a baseball fan. I could have called a cab and made it home in time, but I didn't. When the last out was made we all clapped and hugged and jumped around in the middle of the living room. The old women watched us and smiled.

I was still floating when I got home a little while later to find Emily watching the postgame celebration. But I regret not seeing that final out with her.

We started dating in January of 2002, and at first she was amused by how much I cared about the Yankees. Then alarmed. She couldn't understand how I could lose sleep over baseball. We once saw a friend's baby crying and I said, "That's how I am after the Yanks lose."

"Yeah," said Emily, "in April."

The years passed and she learned more about the game and started to enjoy it on her own. She listened to "her friends" John Sterling and Suzyn Waldman call the game on the radio on her ride home from work, and I'd come home to find her on the couch with the game on, eager to catch me up on what'd happened. She wore t-shirts of her favorite players—Jason Giambi, Jorge Posada, Hideki Matsui, and later, Curtis Grand-erson, Derek Jeter, and her hero, Francisco Cervelli. We didn't share the same interest in movies or music or even books, but go figure, she loved baseball. Every guy should be so lucky.

After Todd Drew died, his wife Marsha left New York, but she kept their season tickets for the first three years of the new stadium. Emily and I went half a dozen times each season, watching games in what would have been Todd's seats, high in the sky behind home plate. Emily was righteous about what it means to be a true fan: you never arrive late and you don't leave early, you don't get up in the middle of a pitch, and you watch the game on the field instead of talking (or texting) on your phone. We saw a first round playoff game in 2009, and the lifeless atmosphere dismayed Em. I told her that after all these years of success, playoff crowds at Yankee Stadium don't get energized until later in October. She said that was horseshit. I didn't disagree.

A couple of seasons later she got her playoff rush. Except it was in July. We picked our games from Marsha at the beginning of each season, usually opting for Saturday afternoon. It was by chance that we found ourselves at the park on July 9, 2011 as the Yanks played the Rays and Derek Jeter entered the game with 2,998 career hits.

The countdown to 3,000 had played out all week. On Thursday night, Jeter made the last out of the game with the Yanks down by four runs. Emily wanted to witness his big hit in person, and I could swear she rooted him to draw a walk or reach on an error in that moment. Or even make an out. He hit a weak grounder to third, the game ended, and she pretended to be disappointed, but I knew better.

The next day it rained. Em was at work. She called and said, "I smell a rain out," and sure enough her wish was granted and the game was postponed.

So there we were on a sunny afternoon in July, behind home plate in the Todd Drew box seats. The place roared when Jeter came to bat in the first inning. He worked the count full against the Rays' ace, David Price, and then singled through the left side of the infield.

"He's going to do it," said Emily.

In his next at bat, on another 3-2 pitch, Jeter got his 3,000th hit. When the ball came off the bat we could tell it was going to go over the fence. It's hard to remember exactly what happened next apart from ten minutes of pleasure. I picked up my wife and hugged her, slapped fives with everyone within reach. Emily teared up, she was so overcome by the moment, and was surprised that they stopped the game to honor the Yankee captain. I thought of Todd, imagined he was there with us, and clapped like he would, until my hands were red.

Of course, Jeter wasn't done. He got three more hits, including the game-winner in the 8th. Then we had the pleasure of watching Mariano Rivera jog in from the bullpen to Metallica's "Enter Sandman" and see him retire the Rays in order to end the game. I've never rooted for a team that has provided more joy than the Yankees have since the mid-'90s. To be there for Jeter's achievement, a Yankee win topped off by Rivera's save,— and to witness it while sitting in Todd's seats with my wife was sweet. And it made up for missing the World Series with her. Our favorite Stadium memory, and it's not even close.

CONTRIBUTORS

MAURY ALLEN was a lifelong sportswriter, author, and commentator with forty published books to his credit and more than two million printed words available for scrutiny. He started as a childhood fan of his native Brooklyn Dodgers and covered the Yankees for more than thirty years for the *New York Post*. Like Babe Ruth, he believed baseball is the only game that really matters.

ED ALSTROM is living out a childhood dream as the organist at Yankee Stadium. He was hired in 2004 to replace the late, great Eddie Layton. Alstrom is a prominent freelance musician in the New York area and has performed with many top names in many famous places. His myriad accomplishments, available CDs, and current activities are always noted at www.edalstrom.com.

MARTY APPEL attended his first Yankee Stadium game in 1956 and worked for the team from 1968–92, first in PR and then as TV producer. He now runs Marty Appel Public Relations and is the author of the recent biography, *Munson: The Life and Death of a Yankee Captain* (Doubleday).

KEVIN BAKER has been a Yankees fan since 1966, when he saw Horace Clarke hit a home run at the old, old Yankee

Stadium. He is a novelist and historian and lives in Manhattan, where every year he visits the site where home plate was in Hilltop Park.

ALLEN BARRA wrote about sports for the *Wall Street Journal* and the *Village Voice*. His latest book is *Yogi Berra: Eternal Yankee* (W. W. Norton). He also wrote, under the pen name Norman Mailer, *The Naked and the Dead*.

MAGGIE BARRA is currently an undergraduate student studying film at Montclair. . . . She was successfully raised as a Yankee fan from an early age in New Jersey and was brought to her first game when she was six years old. She has photo credits on American Heritage.com and in the book *Yogi Berra: Eternal Yankee*.

TED BERG is the senior editorial producer of SNY.tv, where he writes the popular TedQuarters blog. He likes Taco Bell, funk music, and television, and feels uncomfortable writing about himself in the third person like this.

TOM BOSWELL has worked in sports at his hometown *Washington Post* since graduating from Amherst in 1969, starting as a copy boy and becoming a columnist in 1984, focusing on his passion for baseball, golf, and Washington sports. He has published seven books, including the classic compilations *How Life Imitates the World Series* and *Heart of the Game,* won or done most of the usual things, and received the Eugene Meyer Award, the *Post's* highest career-achievement honor. He lives in Maryland with his wife Wendy and two dogs when he isn't sneaking off to play golf with their son Russell, who attends the University of Maryland.

PETE CALDERA grew up a Mets fan, but saw the Yankees play at Shea Stadium in 1974—regrettably missing the old Stadium by a year. He has covered baseball at the *Bergen Record* since 2000, first on the Mets beat. He has been the Yankees beat writer at the paper since 2003 and is a past chairman of the New York chapter of the Baseball Writers' Association.

CLIFF CORCORAN is the co-author of Bronx Banter and a regular contributor to SportsIllustrated.com and the Baseball Prospectus annual. He also contributed to the Baseball Prospectus books *It Ain't Over* and *Mind Game* and twice served as the annual's in-house editor. He edited Howard Bryant's *Juicing the Game* and Brad Snyder's *A Well-Paid Slave,* among others, during his eight years at Viking Books. Before joining Bronx Banter, he was a music critic, lead singer, and blogged about baseball at Clifford's Big Red Blog. He is now a stay-at-home dad in northern New Jersey.

BOB COSTAS started his career calling the exploits of Marvin "Bad News" Barnes for the St. Louis Spirit of the ABA and worked his way to become the most famous sports broadcaster in America. Along the way, he has been a major presence in TV coverage of the NFL, NBA, and MLB, and he has been the face of NBC's Olympics coverage for the better part of twenty years. Costas currently calls games and hosts original programming for the MLB Network.

RICHARD BEN CRAMER was a reporter for the *Baltimore Sun* and won a Pulitzer Prize in 1979 for international reporting at the *Philadelphia Inquirer.* He went on to be a contributor to *Rolling Stone* and *Esquire* and later wrote a highly-celebrated account of the 1988 presidential election, *What it Takes: The Way to the White House.* His classic, and classically profane, profile on Ted Williams for *Esquire,* later published in book form, is the seminal piece on Williams. Cramer's 2000 effort,

Joe DiMaggio: A Hero's Life, was a best-seller and one of the great, uncompromising jock biographies of them all.

NEIL DEMAUSE is a Brooklyn-based journalist and co-author of the book *Field of Schemes: How the Great Stadium Swindle Turns Public Money into Private Profit*. He runs the sports stadium news site FieldofSchemes.com. A Mets fan until the horrors of the Doug Flynn years, he fled to the Bronx just in time for the Yankees' longest postseason drought since they were the Highlanders. He has personally witnessed seven World Series games, two no-hitters, the Pine Tar Game, and the Jeffrey Maier Game, but has still never caught a foul ball.

JON DEROSA lives and works in New York City and writes about baseball for Bronx Banter. He still plays hardball and hasn't entirely lost that sweet lefty swing he developed while playing for his college team at Georgetown. He looks forward to the day when his sons ask him what it was like to watch Mariano Rivera pitch.

MARSHA DREW learned the game of baseball from her husband, Todd. She found out that her grandfather was at Don Larsen's perfect game only after she overheard Todd talking to him about it. Todd and Marsha were married for seventeen years.

TODD DREW started writing about baseball in late 2006 on his Yankees for Justice baseball blog. Todd believed in "baseball and an equally free, open, just society for everyone." He wrote for Bronx Banter in 2008. Todd grew up near Syracuse, New York, but felt more at home in New York City. Todd missed only a handful of Yankee games from June 2002 to the last game at the old Stadium. He would take a half day off for mid-week day games and then go back to the office after the game.

DIANE FIRSTMAN is a lifelong New Yorker and baseball fan. Her master's thesis in quantitative analysis took the principles of *The Hidden Game of Baseball* and applied them to the mid-1980s New York Mets. Prior to joining Bronx Banter, she wrote at Baseball Toaster and had her own blog, Diamonds are for Humor, at MLB.com. When not following the national pastime, she enjoys competitive Scrabble and humor writing.

STEVEN GOLDMAN writes the Pinstriped Bible column for YES. He is the senior-ranking Yankee analyst of the on-line generation and the author of *Forging Genius: The Making of Casey Stengel*. When he is not watching Preston Sturges movies, reading Pogo, or listening to Fats Waller, Goldie is a contributing editor at SBNation, where he writes about baseball history. He writes fiction, has a wife and two kids, and still manages to blog about politics at WholesomeReading.com.

LUIS GUZMAN is one of the most recognizable character actors of his generation, but in New York City—especially uptown— he's most loved for his role as Pachanga, the guy who double-crossed Pacino with Benny Blanco from the Bronx in *Carlito's Way*. A social-worker-turned-actor, Luis was also wonderful in *Q&A*, *Boogie Nights*, *Traffic*, and *The Limey*, but that's not being fair. He's pretty much good in everything he's in, a Latin Marty Balsom.

PETE HAMILL is a son of Brooklyn who, not unexpectedly, loved the Ebbets Field version of the Dodgers and continues to hate the Yankees. Between games, he found time to read newspaper legends like Jimmy Cannon, Murray Kempton, and Meyer Berger, run their prose around in his head, and come out with a voice distinctly his own. Hamill was a memorable city columnist for the *Post* and the *Daily News*, and he was editor of both papers, too. His other writing includes novels and screenplays, but it was with his memoir, *A Drinking Life*, that he reached new heights.

Johnette Howard is a writer and author whose work has been collected in eight anthologies, including *The Best American Sports Writing of the Century*. She still believes her childhood hero, Roberto Clemente, who played for Pittsburgh at Yankee Stadium in the 1960 World Series, is the most graceful baseball player who ever lived.

David Israel burst to prominence in the mid-seventies as a twenty-two-year-old sports columnist for the *Washington Star*. He went on to write a sports column for the *Chicago Tribune* and a general interest column for the *Los Angeles Herald-Examiner* before becoming a writer and producer of TV dramas, mini-series, and movies of the week. He was chairman of the Los Angeles Coliseum Commission during its most recent attempt to bring the NFL back to the city.

Jay Jaffe is a third-generation Dodger fan who's still spooked by a diving Graig Nettles but was later seduced by the dark side upon moving to New York in the mid-nineties. As the founder of the nine-year-old Futility Infielder website (www.FutilityInfielder.com), Jay is an O.B.—Original Blogger. His writing is marked by humor, intelligence, and a deep love for the history of the game, and his writing about the Hall of Fame has become the industry standard. Jay is a columnist for Baseball Prospectus, and his work has appeared on ESPN.com, SI.com, and Salon.com. Oh, and he once finished third in the famous Milwaukee Brewers sausage race.

Marilyn Johnson is the author of a book about the librarian subculture, *This Book Is Overdue!* (Harper, 2010) and another about the cult of obituaries, *The Dead Beat* (HarperPerennial, 2007). She has another identity, as Mrs. Fleder of the Fledermice of the original Rotisserie Baseball League, but she has not let that spoil her love of the game.

Pat Jordan was a bonus baby pitching prospect for the Milwaukee Braves who flamed out fast and later wrote a classic memoir about it, *A False Spring*. He has written eight other books, including a second memoir, *A Nice Tuesday*, and is in his sixth decade as a career freelance magazine writer. Most often seen in the pages of the *New York Times Magazine*, Jordan's work has also appeared everywhere from *Sports Illustrated, GQ, Playboy,* and *Harper's,* to *Woman's Wear Daily, TV Guide,* Deadspin.com, and *AARP The Magazine*. He refers to himself as "The Last Knight of the Freelance," wears Hawaiian shirts, smokes cigars, carries a handgun in his man purse, and still uses a typewriter.

Tyler Kepner covered the Yankees for the *New York Times* from 2002 through 2009. He has also covered the Angels for the *Press-Enterprise* in Riverside, California, the Mariners for the *Seattle Post-Intelligencer*, and the Mets for the *Times*. A native of Philadelphia and a graduate of Vanderbilt University, Tyler is now the national baseball writer and columnist for the *Times*.

Jonah Keri has covered baseball and basketball for the *Wall Street Journal, New York Times, ESPN.com, Bloomberg Sports, Baseball Prospectus, Penthouse* (yes, *Penthouse*), and many other publications. He's also a stock market writer for *Investor's Business Daily*. His new book, *The Extra 2%: How Wall Street Thinking Took a Major League Baseball Team from Worst to First,* drops Spring 2011 (ESPN Books/Ballantine).

George Kimball spent thirty-five years in Boston, ten with the *Phoenix* and twenty-five with the *Herald*, and reckons trying to keep up with Bill Lee in those years took another thirty years off his life expectancy. He passed away in 2011. *Four Kings:*

Leonard, Hagler, Hearns, Duran and the Last Great Era of Boxing was his final book.

DAVE KINDRED became a sportswriter the first time he saw a 90 mile-per-hour fastball. That enabled him to have breakfast with Katarina Witt, lunch with Tiger Woods, and dinner with Stan Musial. Not to mention that night in the moonlight with Charlize Theron.

BOB KLAPISCH has covered baseball in New York for the *Post*, *Daily News,* and, since 1996, the *Bergen Record.* He has also been a regular contributor at ESPN.com and most recently at FoxSports.com. The author of five books—including *Champs: The Diary of the 1996 Yankees*—Klapisch was voted among the nation's top ten columnists by the Associated Press Sport Editors.

TONY KORNHEISER is best known these days for his work on ESPN's "Pardon the Interruption." but before he stepped in front of the cameras, he was one of America's foremost sports-writers and a specialist in the long feature stories known as takeouts. His byline graced the *Washington Post*, the *New York Times,* and *Newsday* as well as magazines ranging from *Inside Sports* to *Street & Smith's Basketball Yearbook.*

MARK LAMSTER writes about the arts and culture. He is the author of *Spalding's World Tour*, an acclaimed history of nine-teenth-century baseball, and is co-founder of the baseball blog YFSF.org. His writing has appeared in the *New York Times*, the *Los Angeles Times*, the *Wall Street Journal*, and many other publications. He is currently at work on a biography of the architect Philip Johnson.

JANE LEAVY is the author of *The Last Boy: Mickey Mantle and the End of America's Childhood,* (HarperCollins, September

2010), the *New York Times* bestseller, *Sandy Koufax: A Lefty's Legacy*, and the comic novel, *Squeeze Play*. She lives in Washington, DC.

BRUCE MARKUSEN is a regular contributor to Bronx Banter and the author of seven books on baseball, including the award-winning *A Baseball Dynasty: Charlie Finley's Swingin' A's*, the recipient of the Seymour Medal from the Society for American Baseball Research. Bruce works as a museum teacher at the National Baseball Hall of Fame, the Farmers' Museum, and the Fenimore Art Museum, all located in Cooperstown, where he lives with his wife, Sue, and their daughter, Madeline.

ANTHONY McCARRON has been covering sports since 1989, first at the *Greenwood (SC) Index-Journal*, now at the *New York Daily News*. The second-banana half of a sportswriting duo—his wife, Judy Battista, covers the NFL for the *New York Times*—he has been writing about baseball since 1999.

JOHN C. McGINLEY worked for a long time as an actor before he made a handsome living at it. He's an indelible part of the early Oliver Stone movies in the eighties, like *Platoon*, *Wall Street* and *Talk Radio*. He was great in the cult classic *Office Space* and later found lasting success on NBC's *Scrubs*. He is a huge Yankee fan.

LEIGH MONTVILLE has been a sportswriter roughly since John McGraw first spit tobacco juice in the Polo Grounds dugout. He has worked for the *New Haven Journal-Courier*, the *Boston Globe*, *Sports Illustrated*, and now writes books about people like Babe Ruth and Ted Williams. He was recently elected to the National Sportscasters and Sportswriters Hall of Fame.

WILLIAM NACK was one of *Sports Illustrated*'s premier writers for more than two decades. He was born in Chicago, educated at the University of Illinois, and spent eleven years as a reporter, sportswriter, and columnist at *Newsday* before moving to *SI*. He is the author of three books, *Secretariat*, *Ruffian*, and *My Turf*, a collection of his magazine journalism.

ROB NEYER has written more words for ESPN.com than anyone still living. Or so his mom says. His mom also says that he's authored, all by himself, six books about baseball, including three entries in the *Big Book of Baseball* series and *The Neyer/James Guide to Pitchers*. Today, Neyer is doing his best to make blogging a respectable profession.

JEFF PEARLMAN is a take-no-prisoners columnist for SI.com and a funny and caustic blogger at JeffPearlman.com. He first achieved notoriety as the author of a controversial article about John Rocker for *Sports Illustrated*, and later went on to write the bestsellers *Boys will Be Boys* and *The Bad Guys Won!* He has also written biographies of Roger Clemens and Barry Bonds as well as worked as a columnist for ESPN.com and *Newsday*.

DAYN PERRY is the author of *Reggie Jackson: The Life and Thunderous Career of Baseball's Mr. October*. A Mississippi native, he now lives in Chicago with his wife, son, and dog. He is duty-bound to remind you that his favorite team, the St. Louis Cardinals, has won three out of five World Series encounters with the Yankees.

CHARLES P. PIERCE—Charlie to his friends—devotes the bulk of his time to writing about politics and the decline of the republic for *Esquire*. It was as a sportswriter, however, that Pierce first made readers pay attention to his chewy language, clear thinking, and refusal to suffer fools. The chops he developed at the *Boston Phoenix* and the *Boston Herald* made him a staple on the bigger stages provided by *the National Sports Daily*,

GQ, and *Sports Illustrated*. There have been books, too, about the nation's new booboisie, about Tom Brady, about his father's battle with Alzheimer's. From the last of those came his entry about the Stadium.

JOE POSNANSKI is a writing cyborg who enthusiastically waxes eloquent on everything from Stan Musial and Albert Pujols to Jerry Seinfeld and co-ed doubles Swedish meatball tossing. He's been an award-winning columnist for the *Kansas City Star*, a virtuoso blogger, and is currently a star feature writer for *Sports on Earth*. Pos might be the only major baseball writer who is equally respected in the press box and in SABR-minded chat rooms on-line. He's also the author of *The Soul of Baseball*, *The Machine*, and *Paterno*.

SCOTT RAAB is a graduate of Cleveland State University and the University of Iowa's Writers' Workshop. He has been a Writer At Large for *Esquire* magazine since 1997. He lives in New Jersey with his wife and son.

ED RANDALL has been a fixture on the New York City sports scene for more than thirty years, dating back to the Sports Channel days in the 1980s. He was the host of the TV program *Ed Randall's Talking Baseball* and still hosts a show by the same name on WFAN radio where he's interviewed a who's who of baseball greats and near-greats. He is the author of several books, including *More Tales from the Yankee Dugout*.

PETER RICHMOND'S most recent book, *The Glory Game*, co-authored with Frank Gifford, was a *New York Times* best-seller. His work has appeared in such publications as *The New Yorker*, *Vanity Fair*, *GQ*, *Rolling Stone* and the *New York Times*

Magazine. He is currently writing a book about the Oakland Raiders of the 1970s.

RAY ROBINSON had a long career as a magazine editor and later authored acclaimed biographies of Christy Mathewson, Will Rogers, and Lou Gehrig. He is the author of numerous books, including *Yankee Stadium: Drama, Glamor, and Glory* (co-written by Christopher Jennison) and lives in New York City.

KEN ROSENTHAL is the senior baseball writer for FoxSports .com. He also is the field reporter for the weekly *MLB on Fox* broadcasts and an insider for the MLB Network. A 1984 graduate of the University of Pennsylvania, he spent thirteen years at the *Baltimore Sun* as a baseball writer and columnist before moving to *The Sporting News* in 2000 and then Fox in 2005.

STEVE RUSHIN was a longtime reporter for *Sports Illustrated.* His Air and Space column ran from 1998 to 2007. He is also the author of three books, including *Road Swing: One Fan's Journey Into the Soul of America's Sports* and *The Pint Man*, a novel. He is married to former basketball player Rebecca Lobo and lives in Connecticut with their three children.

JOHN SCHULIAN was a highly-regarded sports columnist for *the Chicago Sun-Times* before he moved on to Hollywood and became, among other things, a co-creator of TV's *Xena: Warrior Princess*. A special contributor to *Sports Illustrated*, he is the author of two collections of his journalism, *Twilight of the Longball Gods* and *Writer's Fighters and Other Sweet Scientists.*

ALAN SCHWARZ was a longtime senior writer at *Baseball America* before joining ESPN and then the *New York Times* as a reporter and features writer. Schwarz distinguished himself at the *Times* with a series of articles on sport-related brain injuries.

He is also the author of two books, including a terrific history of statistics in baseball, *The Numbers Game*.

EMMA SPAN grew up in New Jersey under the impression that Don Mattingly was God and never fully got over the resulting confusion. She's written about baseball for the *Village Voice*, Slate. com, and the *New York Press*, as well as a wide variety of Web sites. Her first book, *90% of the Game Is Half Mental: And Other Tales From the Edge of Baseball Fandom*, was published in 2010. She lives in Brooklyn with a well-intentioned Labrador.

GLENN STOUT is the author of the text for *Yankees Century*, *Red Sox Century*, *The Cubs*, *The Dodgers*, and has served as series editor of *The Best American Sports Writing* since its inception. He lives in Vermont.

The first game **MIKE VACCARO** ever saw in Yankee Stadium was the second game ever played at the renovated Stadium in April 1976. Though he grew up rooting for the Mets, he retained a deep respect for the Yankees, especially their home. As a writer for the *Newark Star-Ledger* and, since 2002, the *New York Post*, he has covered hundreds of games there—and enjoyed every inning.

HANK WADDLES lives 2,807 miles from Yankee Stadium with his wife and three children. When he isn't obsessing about the Yankees, he teaches eighth-grade English and writes about fatherhood at ShotgunDaddy.com.

For **NATHAN WARD**, the old Yankee Stadium really died with the "1918" chant, which had escorted him (and his Sox cap) down the exit ramps after so many games through the years of the rivalry, from the July 3, 1978, "M-80" game to the Clemens-Pedro showdown. His book, *Dark Harbor: The War for the New York Waterfront* (Farrar, Straus & Giroux) was published this past June.

WILL WEISS has written the Yankee Panky column at Bronx Banter, analyzing media coverage of the team, since 2007. Before joining the Banter lineup, he helped launch YESNetwork.com and served as senior editor from 2002 to 2006. His essay on the greening movement in Major League Baseball appeared in *Baseball Prospectus 2007*, and he was a co-editor of the *2006 Baseball Prospectus Annual*. Will lives on Long Island with his wife and daughter.

JOSH WILKER is the author of *Cardboard Gods: An All-American Tale Told Through Baseball Cards* (Seven Footer Press). He continues to cling to his childhood baseball cards for dear life at CardboardGods.net. He lives in Chicago.

VIC ZIEGEL spent half a century making sure his readers realized that fun was an acceptable part of the games their heroes played. He is best known as a sports columnist for the New York *Daily News* but was also the *News'* sports editor for five years and, before that, a baseball and boxing writer for the *New York Post* and a regular contributor to *Sport, Inside Sports, Esquire,* and *Rolling Stone*. When he and Lewis Grossberger wrote *The Non-Runner's Book,* Ziegel got to tell the world about one of his favorite pastimes: warming down.

DAVE ZIRIN was Press Action's 2005 and 2006 Sportswriter of the Year and has been called by Robert Lipsyte "the best sportswriter in the United States." He writes about sports for *The Nation* magazine and is their first sportswriter in 150 years of existence. He is also the host of XM satellite's popular weekly show, "Edge of Sports Radio." Zirin's new book is *A People's History of Sports in the United States,* part of Howard Zinn's People's History series for the New Press.

ACKNOWLEDGMENTS

This book would have never been made without the blessing and enthusiastic support of Marsha Drew. It is for her, and her extended family, for Todd's family, for Todd and Marsha's co-workers and friends. This collection is our humble way to remember Todd, a token of what he means to us. It's a book of intermingling tastes and sensibilities that celebrates New York's quintessential diversity.

First up, thanks go to Diane Firstman, who came up with the idea of a collection of the Yankee Stadium memories. Good lookin', Dee! Mark Weinstein from Skyhorse knows and cares about good sports books, not to mention music, and was a pleasure to work with.

Of course, my wingman at the Banter, Cliff Corcoran, offered his counsel and editorial expertise freely and his input was appreciated muchly. Will Weiss, another longtime Banter writer, was helpful too, reading pieces and offering sharp insights. The rest of the crew always had my back, and I'm so thankful to be working with the likes of Emma Span, Hank Waddles, Jon DeRosa, and Bruce Markusen. At SNY, Matt Cerrone and Fred Harner have been terrific.

The book you hold in your hands would not be the same without the yeoman efforts of John Schulian, who is flat-out one of the best people I know. The guy is such a mensch he got his famous sportswriter friends to contribute essays, and these are the All Pros we're talking about. He also read drafts, offered advice, and provided essential guidance. John, you are a scholar and prince, and I thank you for your friendship.

I also had help and encouragement along the way from Ray Robinson, Rob Fleder, Glenn Stout, Ben Belth, Dee Shapiro, Donny Fried, Leon Avelino, Steven Goldman, Ted Berg, Jay Jaffe, Jesse Garcia, William Jackson, and Sharon Davis.

In addition I would like to acknowledge the efforts, talents and generosity of Ray Negron, Peter Zanardi, Hart Brachen, Phil Pepe, Greg Prince, Jack Curry, Will Leitch, Roger Kahn, Joe Sheehan, Perry Barber, Chris DeRosa, Mark Feinsand, Dick Lally, Jake Luft, Jon Weisman, Brian Gunn, Kat O'Brein, Cecilia Tan, Bob Timmerman, Will Carroll, Ben Kabak, Tim Marchman, Charles Euchner, Joe Janish, Steve Lombardi, Pete Abraham, Repoz, David Pinto, Carl Biljiak, Alex Ciepley, John Flaherty, Mark Kram, S.L. Price, and Gary Smith. Thank you all so much.

Most special thanks go to my wife, Emily, who actually prefers the new Yankee Stadium to the old one because the upper deck isn't as steep and she can watch a game up there without feeling woozy. Little Miss Treebark McHealthfruit has even taken to eating a hot dog at the new place, proving once again that anything is possible. She is my rock, my biggest cheerleader, and a damn fine editor to boot. Also, my best friend. Yup, I got it good.

Last of all, I want to give a huge shout out to the entire community of regulars at Bronx Banter, from the lurkers to the gabbers (and you know who you are), thanks for coming by and coming back—you keep the banter elevated.

ABOUT THE EDITOR

In 2002, Alex Belth created Bronx Banter, a lifestyle blog about living in New York City and rooting for the Yankees. Before settling in as a cultural explorer, Alex worked in the post-production end of the film business for the likes of Ken Burns, Woody Allen, and the Coen brothers. He has contributed to SI.com and is the author of *Stepping Up: The Story of All-Star Curt Flood and His Fight for Baseball Players' Rights*, as well as the editor of *The Best Sports Writing of Pat Jordan*. His story on George Kimball is featured in "The Best American Sports Writing 2012." The *Village Voice* voted Belth the best sports writer in New York and called Bronx Banter "a New York Treasure."

Also by Alex Belth:

Stepping Up: The Story of All-Star Curt Flood and His Fight for Baseball Players' Rights

The Best Sports Writing of Pat Jordan (Editor)